KT-169-986

The

CLASSIC STEAM

Collection

LES NIXON

Silver Link Publishing Ltd

First published in September 1991
Reprinted November 1992

British Library Cataloguing In Publication Data

Nixon, Les
The classic steam collection
I. Title
625. 2610941

ISBN 0 947971 66 1

Silver Link Publishing Ltd
Unit 5
Home Farm Close
Church Street
Wadenhoe
Peterborough PE8 5TE
Tel/fax (08015) 4-4-0

Typeset by G&M, Raunds, Northamptonshire

Printed and bound in Great Britain

Title page **'A4' No 60024 *Kingfisher* approaches Chaloners Whin Junction, York, with a southbound excursion on 21 May 1966. A panned camera and an exposure of 1/60th second combine to give a superb impression of speed, perhaps one of the best photographic interpretations for Gresley's famous streamlined 'Pacifics'.**

Left **An all-out effort from Stanier Class '5' No 44679 as it battles with the grade at Linthwaite on the climb from Huddersfield to Marsden with a summer SO train for North Wales.**

Author's Introduction

I am told that even as a toddler I was fascinated by trains and I used to bawl my head off when it was time to go home after a pushchair ride down to the lineside.

I suppose my youthful awareness of railways arose because of the strong railway connections of the families of both my mother and father. Indeed, my father, who was a footplateman at Barnsley and Mexborough, moved temporarily to Stratford in the mid-1930s and it was here that he met my mother who was on the clerical staff at Stratford Works.

As a youngster I could always look forward to exotic holidays (at least for the post-war period), courtesy of course of the free travel passes available to my father. Much to the chagrin of my friends who had to be content with Bridlington, Cleethorpes or Mablethorpe, my annual holiday was to the likes of Newquay, Bournemouth and Yarmouth. Sadly though I could never persuade my parents to take a holiday in Peterhead, Stranraer or even Whitley Bay. I used to wonder why! My annual pilgrimage, however, did wonders for my lists of 'cops' of GWR and Southern engines. I was also fortunate enough to enjoy at least one visit each year to grandparents at Billericay, and I came to know the Liverpool Street to Southend line quite well; at least, I was able to recite in the correct order the suburban stations on the Great Eastern main line. This was in the days when most of the trains were in the hands of the handsome Holden 'B12s'. Even today, over 40 years on, I can half close my eyes and see a smoking 'B12' easing off at the top of Wickford Bank and coasting under the two high bridges into Billericay station.

At home, four locations, all within cycling distance, were favourites for spotting trips. Top of the list was undoubtedly Doncaster, followed closely by Leeds, although here most trips were by train — I remember half return privilege tickets bought for 1s 2d. Nearer to home was the Midland main line at Cudworth (of Michael Parkinson fame) or Walton, near Wakefield, where the Midland crossed the East Coast Main Line to Leeds.

If we felt like a day on the footplate, then all we had to do was cycle the 1½ miles to the foot of Worsborough Bank. Here we could enjoy as many rides as we liked on the bankers up the 1 in 40 to the summit at West Silkstone Junction. I came to know these Mexborough-based locomotives intimately; Robinson '04s', 'WDs', Gresley '02s' and of course the famous, or is it infamous, Garratt. My own favourites were without a doubt the '02s' — they used to make such a lovely noise when hard at work, perhaps my earliest appreciation of that delightful Gresley three-cylinder beat. We were, of course, more than keen to get involved in helping to run the engines, and I vividly remember being handed an oil-can on more than one occasion. Many is the time that a scruffy 13-year-old cycled home to an irate mother.

It was at about this time that I took my first photographs of railway subjects; I still have the Box Brownie negatives to this day, out of focus, badly developed, scratched and poorly composed pictures

In the beginning! A picture taken at Canklow shed in the summer of 1949. Classmates pose for the camera on the running plate of a Class '2F' 0-6-0. Over the years I have lost contact with nearly all of them — I wonder where they are now? In the picture are Devaney, Hardy, Hinchliffe, Hudson, King, Lumb, Sunderland, the Profitt brothers and yours truly at the extreme right.

LES NIXON

of locomotives at Worsborough Bank in the summer of 1949. This was to be the state of my photographic capabilities until 1957, when I became the proud owner of a Voigtlander Vito IIa as a 21st birthday present.

Nevertheless my indifferent contact prints of the late '40s and early '50s obviously impressed my schoolfriends who persuaded me to do developing and printing for them too. I recall one occasion when a friend, after his very first trip to Crewe, brought his precious roll of film to me for processing. On it were the latent images of all that Crewe had to offer in the late '40s — 'Patriots', unrebuilt 'Scots' and 'Duchesses'. The film was developed after dark under the kitchen table, see-saw style in a dish of developer. I hadn't even heard of a developing tank then. The result was disastrous — a totally black film. My friend, on being told the news, wasn't at all surprised. He confided that he had already had a quick look at the film and he couldn't see anything on it either!

In common with most of my friends at the time, nearly all the photographs I took were portraits of engines and, more often than not, pictures of rare (to me, that is) named engines. I remember taking no fewer than three photographs in appalling light of my very first Scottish 'Director', *Lord Glenallan*, at Carlisle Canal shed. I did try to take pictures of moving trains but the results were always very disappointing, to say the least. I used to look at the published work of Frank Hebron and E.R. Wethersett and wonder how they managed such superb results. Advice and encouragement was hard to come by in those days. The advent of my 35mm camera, however, certainly resulted in a quantum leap in the quality of my photographs, at least from a sharpness point of view. The f3.5 Color Skopar lens of the Voigtlander was a superb objective.

However, quality action pictures still eluded me and I now realise that my major difficulty was not having access to a darkroom for enlarging work. Contact prints were rather useless, and commercially produced postcards were both of indifferent quality and quite expensive. In 1957 colour transparency photography was in its infancy, but it had the attraction that the results came through the post — at last no printing problems! The difficulty was the cost of the film; £1 18s (£1.90) for a 36-exposure roll. Allowing for inflation, the equivalent price today would be around £20 a film. No wonder a student with limited financial resources didn't take many pictures! The other almost insurmountable problem with colour photography was the speed of the film. Kodachrome 1 was rated at

'8F' No 48104, at the head of a Hunslet–Carlisle freight, is delightfully framed by the sweeping overbridge just to the west of the station at Kirkstall on the former Midland line from Leeds to Shipley. When this photograph was taken in July 1965 all four tracks were still in use, but by this date the level of traffic barely justified retention. Two years later the two tracks on the right were lifted.

Perhaps this was the highlight of a guard's shift on a northbound freight for Carlisle over Shap. An intimate view of the business end of a hard-working banker, in this case BR Class '4' 4-6-0 No 75039, seen here in the early morning light near Scout Green.

just 8 ASA, which meant an exposure of the order of 1/250th at f2.2 even on the brightest summer's day. There was little chance of successful action photography with my f3.5 Vito IIa.

As a result, photography for a period took a back seat to other interests, although, as the odd example in this volume shows, the few pictures which I did take are now treasured.

The end of student days in the early '60s heralded a new phase in my love affair with railways. The main difference, in spite of being newly married, was that at last I had the wherewithal to indulge seriously in the hobby of railway photography. From about 1963 the number of pictures gradually increased, followed in 1964 with a serious reawakening of my interest in monochrome work. Then followed a hectic period of four years recording the all too rapid passing of the steam engine. Inevitably there was remorse at having missed some of the already scrapped classes, and a clear mission (some would say obsession) emerged to record as many of the locomotives and lines as possible before they were either scrapped, closed or modernised. Late in 1965 the trusty Vito IIa was relegated to second division work when I invested in a pair of Exakta Varex 11a SLR bodies. The new cameras introduced me to the world of interchangeable lenses, a move which revolutionised my picture-making opportunities. It also introduced problems too. With hindsight I now realise that for some considerable time I fell into the trap of thinking that *every* picture looked better through a telephoto lens!

Towards the end of this period I formed many lasting friendships with people of kindred interest. I was soon involved in several railway photographic portfolios, and I became a member of the Railway Correspondence and Travel Society. For the first time for 15 years I was able to benefit from the advice of those who had long mastered the art. To them all I owe a particular debt of gratitude. My photography improved by leaps and bounds and culminated in late 1967 with the purchase of my first medium format camera — a 2¼-inch square Minolta Autocord. This proved to be a splendid camera, its principal limitations being the fixed standard lens and the between-the-lens leaf shutter. At best it gave an effective speed of 1/400th second, and that on a good day with the wind behind it, which was fine until you attempted photographing trains travelling at speeds of more than 40 mph. Nonetheless the technical quality of the pictures taken in the last eight months of BR steam was head and shoulders above the rest. Eventually medium format SLRs with focal plane shutters came on to the market, instruments which were absolutely ideal for railway photography even if they were very expensive. I made the decision to switch to the Pentax 6x7 system in 1972 and these cameras continue to give me yeoman service today. It is always easy to be wise after the event, but with hindsight I wish I had raided the piggy bank or found a kind bank manager back in the '50s. . .

Thus far I have made mention only of the technical aspects of the hobby, but another equally important consideration is artistic interpretation. It is well known that until the early 1950s the serious railway photographer concentrated almost exclusively on record aspects. Nothing less than pin-sharp detail would do. No wonder sturdy tripods and plate cameras were the order of the day. Not that there was anything wrong with this approach. Quite the contrary — present-day protagonists of the hobby are indeed delighted by those perfect three-quarter-front studies from the cameras of the likes of H. Gordon Tidey. The move to capture on film the *mood* of steam gained pace in the early '60s and I, along with many others, admired the completely novel approach of several youthful photographers. Foremost among these was perhaps Colin Gifford who, partly through his books *Each a Glimpse* and *Decline of Steam*, gained a deserved reputation for his work. The impact of this avant garde style of photography on my perception of the subject was considerable. Abandoned forever was the thesis that the only good railway pictures were three-quarter-front studies with the sun over the shoulder.

In today's motorway era of fast cars it is relatively easy to enjoy a day's or a weekend's photography in just about any part of the country. How different it was in the past. As mentioned previously, early forays to the lineside were accomplished by cycle or, if we could afford it, by train, and were almost exclusively undertaken in high summer.

Horizons expanded considerably when I bought my first motorbike in 1954, a 197cc Ariel Colt. One of the very first long trips I undertook was a day's ride — yes, a day's ride — from South Yorkshire to Hawick in Southern Scotland, the attraction being the small allocation of Class 'D30' 4-4-0s. The Ariel was the precursor of a series of bikes, all of which did yeoman service until the appearance of my first car in 1962. I have Jekyll and Hyde memories of the Francis Barnett Falcon, the Enfield 350cc Bullet and the BSA A7 Shooting Star. Unfortunately the cost of running the motorbikes (and a girlfriend!) meant that there wasn't a lot left for railway photography. There were lots of trips to sheds on Sundays, but not many worthwhile pictures to show for them. In my garage today is a beautifully restored BSA Shooting Star, and a summer trip on it to Keighley or Loughborough truly takes me back more than 30 years.

It has been both a pleasure and to a degree a chore to produce this book. A pleasure for the revival of memories; a chore for the hard work required in the darkroom to produce reasonable prints from numerous indifferent 35mm negatives. The book has also been the catalyst for a personal tragedy. By early May 1991, only 20 or so negatives remained to be reprinted, and I earmarked the evening of the 3rd for the task. Accordingly my negative collection for 1965/6/7 was loaded into the car while I first drove to Altrincham to take pictures of the 20th birthday celebrations of the introduction of the Class '304' EMUs to the line. While I was on the station for just over an hour, my car and its precious contents were stolen. Sadly at the time of writing these notes, one month on, nothing has been recovered. I continue to hope for the best, but inevitably future perusal of this book will, for me, arouse many, many mixed feelings and memories.

Les Nixon
Hathersage
Sheffield
June 1991

One of the many attractions of the steam locomotive was the huge variety of shape and size, ranging from the humble London & South Western Class 'B4' 0-4-0 dock tank to the mighty LNER Garratt. This trio of pictures presents the contrasting styles of three very different classes. Repeating patterns often make for interesting photographs, as can be seen here.

Left **Isle of Wight Class 'O2' 0-4-0Ts Nos 16 *Ventnor* and 33 *Bembridge* at Ryde St Johns on 23 April 1966.**

Above right **The result of a sympathetic ear and willing hands at West Hartlepool shed in August 1965. At my request, three Class 'Q6' 0-8-0s were manoeuvred into an ideal echelon position outside the straight shed. Unfortunately my prayer to the Almighty for a little sunshine to add the finishing touches to the picture was rather less successful. Note the absence of vacuum brake and steam heat on these locomotives; it was rare indeed to find one of these workhorses on passenger duty.**

Right **Class 'A4s' Nos 60019 *Bittern* and 60034 *Lord Faringdon* at Ferryhill shed, Aberdeen, in August 1966.**

BITTERN
LORD FARINGDON

As noted elsewhere in this book, I spent the weekend of 15-16 January 1966 in the south photographing one of the commemorative runs of the Class 'S15' 4-6-0s. On the long run home to Sheffield I decided to break my journey at Oxford, and where else to pause for a moment's relaxation and reflection but the steam shed? By this date the shed had only just closed and had assumed an air of total abandonment. A large number of locos and bric à brac were there, covered rather appropriately I thought by a light sprinkling of snow. Surprisingly most of the GW locos still carried their number plates.

Left and below left A selection of 13 locomotives, including 'Halls', 'Granges' and a couple of '61XX' 2-6-2Ts, are seen through the broken windows of the coaling stage, while *below left* a loaded tub of coal waits in vain for its next customer with a snow-covered 'Hall' providing the backdrop.

Above right and right Detail of the whistle and dome of an LSWR Class 'O2' 0-4-4T, a locomotive designed by Adams and introduced in 1889.

Trains, and steam locomotives in particular, have had a fascination for generations of children. Platform-end adoration of steam engines was a daily occurrence at every major station throughout the country, and even prompted the famous pre-war Southern Railway poster where a young boy is chatting up the driver of a 'King Arthur' at one of the London termini. These three pictures echo this delightful interface from the past.

Above **The Gresley Class 'P2' 2-8-2s were especially designed for service on the Aberdeen line north of the Border. Sadly I never saw one of these fine engines, for by the time I was old enough to take an intelligent interest in railways they had been rebuilt by Thompson as rather unattractive 'Pacifics' and reclassified 'A2/1'. In their rebuilt form they continued to be allocated to Scottish sheds for a few years and as such were difficult engines to spot by southern enthusiasts.**

In the very early '50s, all six locomotives were transferred south, principally to New England and King's Cross where they tended to be used on secondary duties such as express freights. Surprisingly, in this picture No 60504 *Mons Meg*, about to leave Doncaster with a south-bound express, carries a 34E Neasden shed plate. At the time I paid little attention to this detail but I cannot recall any of these locomotives being allocated to the Great Central line, although they were infrequent visitors. This photograph was taken in the spring of 1955 and was taken with a borrowed Ensign Selfix. The film was 'professionally' developed by the local chemist but not printed properly until the mid-'60s. Note the fireman apparently sweeping the running plate of the loco keenly watched by a schoolboy in the traditional dress of the time.

Above right **Rose Grove station; a young boy and girl cast admiring glances towards two Class '8Fs' Nos 48278 and 48410 as they prepare to move on to the shed on 15 June 1968. Note the gas lamps and the totem station signs.**

Right **Waterloo is the unmistakable location of this scene showing 'Battle of Britain' 'Light Pacific' No 34087 *45 Squadron* about to leave with an eight-coach boat train special for the *Reina del Mar* at Southampton on 16 May 1967.**

WAY OUT

34087

My father and grandfather were footplatemen with, between them, over 60 years of railway service. My father was apt to take a less than romantic view of the steam locomotive — indeed, I recall him saying many years ago that his only regret was that diesels came 25 years too late! He would readily agree to the delights of working steam on pleasant days in the spring and summer months, but he countered these with the questionable delights of working a tender-first '04' into a howling gale and rain at 3 o'clock in the morning in mid-winter. So too was this 'Jekyll and Hyde' attitude prevalent towards shed duties, as depicted in this selection of pictures.

Left It was years before I realised just how crews managed to get into the smokebox of an 'A4'. All was revealed at Ferryhill shed in May 1965. I wonder if the cranks used for the job are now a collector's item? Perhaps one was kept with each locomotive and identified by the engine number.

Left The fireman at Rose Grove was less than enthusiastic about the tasks to be performed on Class '5' No 45394 on shed after a day's work. No doubt he would have been totally dismayed if he had been told that in 25 years time people would volunteer to do his job in their spare time!

Above right On the other hand, the fitter's task was perhaps a little more creative, even though his skills belonged to the big hammer era rather than today's ultra-clean microscopic computer age. Attention to Class '5' No 44947 at Bolton shed clearly required the services of high technology — an oxy-acetylene torch.

Right The driver of BR Standard Class '5' No 73133 attends to the lubrication of the big-end before moving off shed in March 1965. Latterly large numbers of the class were allocated to Patricroft, the location of this photograph. Indeed, by early 1968 even on a Saturday it was not unusual to find as many as 30 of these locomotives on shed, but sadly by then the writing was well and truly on the wall, since most were not in steam and their next journey would be their last — to the scrapyard.

5
44947

5
73133

At one time a major part of the locomotive stock of all but the Southern Railway was the humble shunting tank engine. Most spent their time out of the public eye and were rarely the focus of attention for photographers.

Above **In Derbyshire a nucleus of 0-4-0T and 0-6-0T locomotives were shedded at Barrow Hill, Staveley, primarily to deal with BR traffic within and to and from the Stanton & Staveley works complex. Even in the late '60s, a major part of the works was devoted to iron and steel production, as can be seen in this dramatic industrial backdrop for Johnson 0-6-0T half-cab No 41763 busy shunting near the blast furnaces in April 1965. Surprisingly, access to the works was remarkably free and easy and in many visits I never had anything other than total co-operation from company staff. Fortunately one of these fine locomotives is preserved, and at the time of writing is a long way from home at Swanage in Dorset.**

Above right **The delightful small Deeley 0-4-0Ts, of which No 41528 was an example, were used on the less demanding duties within the works, and served alongside the company's own fleet of industrial locomotives. In this picture the 0-4-0ST on the right nicely complements its British Railways counterpart. It was built by William Bagnall in 1949 (Works No 2907) and carried the unusual name *D.N.T.*, the initials of one of the company directors at the time.**

Right **One of the more unusual latter-day steam developments on British Railways was the construction of further examples of locomotives which had been designed many years earlier. A batch of no fewer than 28 Class 'J72' 0-6-0Ts were built at Darlington between 1949 and 1951, some 52 years after the introduction of the Wilson Worsdell class back in 1898. A similar situation also arose on the London Midland Region when a further small batch of five 0-4-0ST locomotives were delivered in 1953, being a copy of the 1932 Kitson-built locomotives to the design of Sir William Stanier. Minor differences included an extended saddle tank and enlarged bunker to carry an extra ton of coal, both of which required a slight increase in overall length. One of this later batch, No 47006, is pictured alongside the winding house at the top of Sheep Pasture Incline on the Cromford & High Peak Railway in July 1965. The locomotive was sub-shedded here from Rowsley depot and was from time to time worked up and down the incline to its home base. In spite of several attempts I was never fortunate enough to catch the locomotive on one of its transfer movements. It is too late now — today the incline is a footpath.**

41528

47006

Left Smallbrook Junction on the Isle of Wight, about 1 mile to the south of Ryde St Johns, was a truly delightful spot to savour the delights of the Victorian branch-line railway, even as late as 1966. As can be seen, the junction was in the middle of nowhere and some distance from the nearest road. On a still day you could just about hear an 'O2' tank setting off from St Johns and then from time to time momentarily shutting off steam as the driver notched her up on the climb to the junction. When this picture was taken, at Easter 1965, the line to Newport and Cowes was closed and the box temporarily out of use. 0-4-4T No 22 *Brading* rattles past the deserted box with a train of vintage stock bound for Ryde Pier Head. Today the location is once again in the news, with the Isle of Wight Steam Railway extending its tracks to the junction where a brand new interchange station is to be built.

Above The two lines running south to Smallbrook Junction from Ryde St Johns were in fact single lines in parallel, the right track for Newport, the left for Shanklin and Ventnor. Class 'O2' No 22 *Brading*, one of the stalwarts of the island's motive power for many, many years, takes yet another train of vintage stock up the hill for Shanklin on a spring day in 1965. The day, I recall, was perfect for steam photography; crisp, clear light with sufficient nip in the air to give a lovely 'cotton wool' exhaust.

Below An Ivatt Class '2' 2-6-2T ambles along a stretch of the Swanage branch which, in 1991, is, like that at Smallbrook, soon to re-open for traffic. No 41312 is pictured shortly after leaving Corfe Castle with an afternoon Wareham–Swanage local on 25 August 1966.

LES NIXON

Among the last steam-hauled local passenger trains into Sheffield Midland was the 06.45 Chinley to Sheffield and the return 09.39 ex Sheffield. Latterly a small number of Ivatt Class '2' 2-6-0s were allocated to Buxton to cover this duty along with the lightweight freights to Friden on the Cromford & High Peak line. The train usually loaded to three bogies, well within the capabilities of these fine little engines. No 46485, a regular performer on this duty, has steam to spare as it coasts past Hathersage signal box into the station in January 1964.

Above **The Bulleid 'Pacifics' gained a reputation for being 'light on their feet' and any start involving a heavy train and a greasy rail could be guaranteed to produce a spectacular slip or two, or three, or four! Such was the case at Southampton Central on a very damp but bright winter's day in January 1966; 'Battle of Britain' No 34085 *501 Squadron* provides a fine spectacle of steam and smoke as it leaves with a down express for Bournemouth.**

Right **Much has been written in recent years about the Settle & Carlisle line, and in particular the 'Long Drag' from Settle Junction to Blea Moor. Text is perhaps superfluous — pictures speak louder than words. In complete contrast to the football crowds which gather today, I was alone to record the awe-inspiring spectacle of '8F' No 48517 and '9F' 2-10-0 No 92137 flat out at the head of a northbound rail train near Sheriff's Brow on 12 August 1967.**

1Z78
SLS
SPECIAL

75019
75019
75027

Above Tebay was the traditional staging point to attach bankers to heavy northbound trains for the 1 in 75 slog to Shap summit. Oxenholme was, however, often called to provide assisting engines or bankers for the somewhat easier climbs of 1 in 131/106 up Grayrigg. Here Standard Class '4' No 75043 has been attached as pilot to '9F' No 92071 at the head of a particularly heavy northbound freight which eventually paused at Tebay to attach a banker for the final ascent of Shap. The train is pictured approaching Low Gill where the line from Clapham and Sedbergh joined the West Coast Main Line.

In the weeks leading up to the date of the final elimination of steam from British Railways, numerous specials were run to cater for those who wished to celebrate the end of an era in style. The final day of operation, Sunday 11 August 1968, was intended to see the very last steam-hauled train on BR, and accordingly the cost of a ticket for the return run from Liverpool to Carlisle via the Settle & Carlisle line was £15 15s (£15.75). Although this may seem a most reasonable sum today, when inflation is taken into account the price in 1991 terms was around the £130 mark. No wonder it is remembered today as the super-priced 15 guinea special! Photographers had little chance of obtaining masterpieces at this late hour; for a start there were many following the trains by car. However, it was indeed a challenge to work out the maximum number of times you could photograph a train in reasonable locations and with the light at an agreeable angle. As always, trains would run late and throw out even the most carefully laid plans.

Above left On 4 August I was lucky to be one of a group of around a dozen photographers on the approach to Diggle on the former LNWR Standedge route. The sun shone and a nicely groomed pair of Class '5s', Nos 44871 and 44894, hauling an SLS Special, made a fine picture. Readers will note the location of the colour light signal; clearly the Micklefield loop to Stalybridge had, by this date, been closed.

Left BR Standard Class '4' 4-6-0s Nos 75019/27 accelerate away from Hellifield for Skipton with another of the many 'last run' excursions operated in the few weeks before the formal end of steam. No 75019 at the time carried BR lined black livery while No 75027 (now preserved on the Bluebell Railway) was in BR green. The date is 28 July 1968.

48191

Left A slightly easterly wind gathers the exhaust of '8F' No 48191 as it struggles manfully up Norman's Bank on the climb to Edale and Cowburn Tunnel with one of the last steam-hauled freight trains through the Hope Valley in March 1968. The train of Presflos from Blue Circle's cement works at Hope bound for Heaton Mersey was steam-hauled almost to the end of BR steam. The motive power was invariably an '8F' which with a brake-van worked over from Stockport in the late afternoon to turn on the triangle at Dore and Totley and retraced its path back to Earles Sidings at Hope.

Above left Ashington Colliery was one of the major collieries in Northumberland and was the hub of much railway activity on both National Coal Board and British Railways lines. 'J27' No 65789 gets to grips with a trip coal working in the colliery complex.

Above right Today just seven mechanical signal boxes control all traffic over the Settle & Carlisle line. In the '50s and '60s there were seven signal boxes in operation on the section between Settle Junction and Blea Moor alone. Even then it was not unusual at particularly busy times, or when a train was in difficulties on the climb, for a train to be halted part way up the 'Long Drag'. Here, on 4 November 1967, the northward progress of a '9F' had been brought to a halt by the signalman at Selside, while photographers waited with keen anticipation for the spectacular restart. Judging by the smoke it would appear that the fireman was taking the opportunity to knock the fire into shape.

Enthusiasts bemoan the passing of the steam locomotive, and while for me it too was the focal point of interest, as the years pass by I realise more and more that the general railway scene of the period was equally interesting and sadly somewhat under-recorded photographically. Gantries of semaphore signals are perhaps one of the more obvious examples, and I delight in perusing old pictures of our major stations which show veritable forests of signals as far as the eye can see. The skills of the engine crew of yesteryear, particularly on a dark winter's night, are perhaps lightly dismissed in the era of multi-aspect colour light signals viewed from the warmth of the cab of a diesel. Photographically semaphore signals are a superb foil for the steam locomotive, the theme for this selection of pictures.

Above The splendid signal gantry just to the north of Preston was a splendid sentinel of the steam era, and was demolished soon after the end of steam in 1968 to make way for electrification of the West Coast Main Line to Carlisle. No fewer than 32 semaphore signals adorned the gantry when this picture was taken in the summer of 1967, as Class '5' No 45424 eases an engineers' train out of Preston station. Note the three S&T engineers working at the end of the gantry; I suspect that they took a rather less nostalgic view of these relics from the Victorian age.

Below Track enthusiasts will no doubt look at this picture with a degree of disbelief. The complexity of the track layout for a freight-only line indicates that it once must have carried a great deal of traffic. The location is Percy Main (I never knew where this shed, 52E, was in my junior spotting days) and this was the view looking north in March 1967. One of Wilson Worsdell's delightful Class 'J27' 0-6-0s, No 65812, drifts down the hill towards the Tyne with a motley collection of coal wagons. Note the five-plank wooden-bodied wagons next to the locomotive.

Above Leeds was a fascinating railway centre, being a focal point of activity in the north. The principal LMS station, City, was just half a mile from the LNER station at Central, but at Holbeck station two of the principal routes crossed; the main line to King's Cross was carried over the line to Skipton and Carlisle by a steel girder viaduct, which can be seen in the background of this picture with, to the right, part of the station building of Holbeck Upper. The platforms of the abandoned Holbeck Lower are out of sight beyond the signals. On 18 June 1966 BR Standard Class '3MT' 2-6-0 No 77000 struggles to keep a heavy westbound coal train on the move. The viewpoint for this picture was the steps of Wortley Junction signal box. The sidings to the right of the picture served the local gasworks, while the lines on the extreme left curved and climbed to join the main line into Leeds Central. This was the route taken by such prestigious trains as the 'Queen of Scots' on its journey north to Harrogate, Ripon and Darlington. Note the 20 mph speed restriction applicable to the curve at the time.

Right Chester was one city which retained its pre-grouping London & North Western semaphores well into the '60s, and one of the finest gantries was situated alongside the former GWR shed. This silhouette study, featuring an unidentified Stanier 2-6-4T, was photographed on 4 August 1966.

B315203

Left Anyone travelling for the first time by train from Sheffield to the Hope Valley is guaranteed a pleasant surprise. The route passes through Totley tunnel, at 3 miles 950 yards the second longest in the country, and emerges into fresh air at Grindleford station, spectacularly located in superb National Trust scenery just a few yards beyond the western portal. At night the engine crew of local passenger trains could have been excused for overshooting the platform were it not for the loud gong which was automatically operated by the passage of the train when it was a few hundred yards from the tunnel mouth. This is the view into the tunnel from the down platform in March 1965, with 'WD' 2-8-0 No 90189 at the head of an unfitted freight.

Below left At first sight this may seem a distinctly dangerous place for a photographer to be practising his art, but the picture doesn't tell the complete story! This was a shot I had had in mind for some considerable time, but I realised that the only occasion it would be at all practicable was when the line through the tunnel was closed for maintenance work. In the event this photograph was taken just a couple of months after the line through the single-bore Nelson tunnel at Standedge had been officially closed and it was quite safe to stand and wait. Indeed, it was probably the best location to be in, since I recall that it rained for most of that day. It is also my excuse for not doing the gardening of the weeds which can be seen in front of the engine. An unidentified Class '9F' approaches the surviving twin-bore Standedge tunnel with a westbound freight.

Right The 09.39 Sheffield–Chinley local was probably the train I photographed most in the mid-'60s. At that time my office was just five minutes' walk from Sheffield Midland station and many is the time I was 'unavailable for duty' at 09.45. 'Mickey Mouse' Ivatt Class '2' No 46485 emerges from the tunnel under East Bank Road on 20 April 1966. These engines were fitted with either a broad or, as here, a narrow chimney; my own preference was for the former. As one rather blunt Yorkshire friend once put it: 'Those small chimneys don't half give 'em a constipated appearance!'

Below On a bitterly cold and frosty morning, a rather grimy 'Merchant Navy' 'Pacific' emerges from Southampton Tunnel into the sunshine with a Waterloo–Bournemouth express. The locomotive is *Clan Line*, one of 11 of the class to survive the cutter's torch. These days No 35028 is still from time to time in active main-line service, but immaculately turned out with gleaming paint and brasswork. Note the third rail, already in position for the electrification switch-on of June 1967 which spelled the end of steam on the Southern Region.

Right The majority of photographs taken in the Shap area were on the climb between Tebay and Shap summit, in spite of the fact that there were a number of quite excellent locations to the north. On 8 July 1967 I sacrificed the spectacle on trains on the northbound climb for a photographic session at Thrimby. In the shadow of Harrison's limeworks, Class '5' No 45345 scuttles by with the regulator closed at the head of a Blackpool to Glasgow summer Saturday holiday extra. At this time the up loop at Thrimby was still in situ, with the exit controlled by these superb London & North Western lower quadrants. Note the proliferation of telegraph poles, the bane of generations of railway photographers who tried steam photography on Shap in the morning.

Above The preservation movement of today is to be applauded for the recreation of so many near authentic scenes from the past. There are, however, certain images which it can never recapture and one is certainly the shed scene of yesteryear. They were dirty and, to many people, disagreeable places, but above all else they simply oozed atmosphere. Swirling steam and smoke, the fireman shovelling coal into a distant firebox, the gurgle of an injector, the smell of oil and hot steam, water pouring out of wash-out hydrants and, most of all, a parade of travel-stained locomotives. 2-6-4Ts Nos 42152 and 42189 on Manningham shed, Bradford, on 6 April 1966 capture the mood precisely — certainly better than the latter-day B&Q superstore!

LES NIXON

60886

Above left York shed became well known to thousands of latter-day visitors when it was refurbished to become the National Railway Museum. In this moody study, Class 'V2' 2-6-2 No 60886 is highlighted by a shaft of sunlight permeating the murky smoke-filled gloom. Determining the correct exposure was always a problem with subjects like this — indeed, the correct value was often a compromise between that required for the highlights and the deep shadows. At least, as on this occasion, it was possible to make several exposures in the hope that at least one would be correct.

Left Canklow was the last operational steam shed in the Sheffield area. Located on the eastern side of the city on the so-called old road from Rotherham Masborough to Tapton Junction, Chesterfield, it was a typical Midland Railway roundhouse. In my youth it was always known as an LMS shed, 19C, and I never accepted its transfer to Eastern Region jurisdiction when it acquired the code 41D, a sub-shed of Tinsley diesel depot, 41A. Residents on 15 May 1965 included Class 'B1' No 61315 and Class '5' No 45332, the former being prepared for another turn of duty on the Hope Valley local services to Manchester Central.

Above A nostalgic scene depicting the Stygian gloom of the inside of Wolverhampton Oxley shed in December 1964. Surprisingly the windows were sufficiently clean to allow the rays of the sun to highlight a quartet of pannier tanks which included Nos 3776 and 9658. Note the spare buffers and the shovel propped against the tank. Judging by the pile of ashes on the buffer beam, it had no doubt been left there after the fireman had cleaned out the smokebox. In later years I came to know Wolverhampton quite well, since my wife-to-be lived there for a number of years.

Right North Blyth shed was a typical North Eastern roundhouse and home for a large stud of 'J27s' and, latterly, Ivatt Class '4' and Class 'K1' 2-6-0s. The sun pierces the murky gloom in August 1966; waiting for their next turn of duty are Nos 65795 and 65892.

Left At the foot of Shap, a northbound freight train is on the move with BR Standard Class '4' No 75032 pushing hard. Of interest is the goods yard in the middle distance, marking the route of the former North Eastern line to Kirkby Stephen. Today the M6 motorway crosses the railway at Tebay at this precise point.

Above At an altitude of 969 feet, Peak Forest was the summit of the Midland Railway's main line between Derby and Manchester, an obstacle which presented significant operating difficulties, not least for latter-day limestone trains from the ICI quarries at Tunstead bound for the chemical plants at Northwich in Cheshire. Bankers were required for the 2 miles of 1 in 90 to Peak Forest, a duty performed by Buxton '8Fs' for many years. In this picture a loaded train straddles the summit and eases off steam for the long 17-mile descent to Cheadle Heath while the banker drops off the tail to return to Tunstead.

Right For years banking locomotives stood at Todmorden, the start of the climb to Copy Pit summit, waiting to assist freight trains bound for the Preston area of Lancashire. Towards the end of steam these turns were an easy option for footplate crews since the level of traffic had dwindled to such an extent that only one or two trips per shift were required. On a beautiful sunny winter's day in December 1966 I waited in vain for over 3 hours for some activity, and the only picture I took was this one showing a pair of very inactive Stanier '8Fs' waiting patiently in the loop near Stansfield Hall Junction. Patience is indeed one of the prime requirements of the aspirant railway photographer!

The nearest focal point of freight activity close to home is the small but intensively used yard at Earles Sidings, Hope. Indeed, the yard has never been quite large enough, certainly in recent years, to effectively handle all the traffic on offer, and it was common practice to temporarily stable trains in sidings at the nearby stations of Edale, Bamford and Grindleford. Earles Sidings are situated about 3 miles up the 7-mile bank from Bamford to the summit at Cowburn Tunnel, and consequently westbound trains from the yard are faced with a long gruelling climb, much of it at 1 in 100. There is certainly no opportunity to get a run at the bank, and steam-hauled trains often took 20 minutes to clear the summit. This picture emphasises the delightful rural setting of the yard, and shows a rather run-down class '8F', No 48115, making a noisy departure on 18 April 1968. On this occasion progress was so slow that the train could have been successfully chased on a bicycle!

Above I hope readers will excuse any undue emphasis on pictures taken in the Tebay/Shap area in this book, but in defence — if indeed defence is necessary — it was undoubtedly one of the best places in the north to see and hear steam hard at work. On more than one occasion I pitched a tent for the weekend in the delightful copse just opposite Scout Green signal box, and this was the view in prospect from my camp-bed by just flipping the fly-sheet to one side. As you can see it was a delightful scene by day (except when it was pouring with rain), but truly spectacular at night. Somehow one didn't mind being woken up in the middle of the night as yet another freight, complete with its own pyrotechnic display, blasted its way to the summit. Here BR Standard Class '4MT' 4-6-0 No 75039 is being pushed to the limit — as indeed was the fireman, judging by the fact that the locomotive is blowing off — at the tail-end of a freight on 17 June 1967. The train locomotive, incidentally, wasn't photographed, and my notebook gives me the reason — it was a Brush Type 4 diesel, or Class 47 in today's language.

Right Latter-day enthusiasts regret the passing of first generation DMUs, but it doesn't seem so long ago that the current fashion was to bemoan the demise of many pre-Grouping branch-line locomotives in favour of the ubiquitous and often disliked BR Standard Class '4MT' 2-6-4T. Such was the case on the Brockenhurst–Lymington branch, where the casualties were the ex-LSWR 'M7' 0-4-4TS. Looking somewhat ungainly, No 80085, bereft of front number plate, ambles through the woods near Buckland with a train for Brockenhurst in July 1967.

Left The task of finding locomotive sheds, and more importantly identifying the buses necessary to get you there, was made so much easier in the late 1940s and 1950s when F/Lt A.C.F. Fuller published his invaluable *The British Locomotive Shed Directory* in December 1947. I still have a mint copy in my possession (priced 7s 6d) which instructs me to take a Salford Corporation No 67 (Peel Green) bus in Bridge Street to take me to Patricroft shed (alighting at Franklin Street). A journey in the summer of 1967 would almost certainly have produced a scene like this, depicting BR Class '5' No 73135 beneath the shadow of the coaling tower.

Below Staveley GC shed was located to the south of Staveley Town station. On 5 June 1965 locomotives on shed included 'WD' 2-8-0 No 90277, Robinson '04/3' No 63701 and Class 'O1' 2-8-0 No 63863.

Above Dundee Tay Bridge shed looking north, featuring the tail-end of a 'B1' tender and Class 'J37' No 64577.

Below Goosehill Junction signal box at Normanton was at one time one of the busiest in rural South Yorkshire, controlling movements on the busy Midland Leeds–Sheffield main line and the L&Y line through to Wakefield Kirkgate and the Calder Valley. This was the scene looking south in July 1964. The signalman, just visible in the box, has obviously yet to make his mind up about the destination of the 'WD', while an Ivatt Class '4' 2-6-0 is held at the signals waiting for a local passenger train ahead of it to clear the section. Today the junction has gone completely, and two tracks only remain to Wakefield.

Right Newton Heath-based 'Jubilee' No 45632 *Tonga* waits patiently for the right away at New Mills South Junction with a freight from nearby Gowhole yard. Gowhole was the major Midland Railway goods railhead for much of north-east Derbyshire, south-east Lancashire and parts of Cheshire. It was also a major interchange point for trans-Pennine traffic which originated from south Yorkshire and north-east Derbyshire, traffic which in the '50s regularly brought LMS Garratts to the yard via the Hope Valley route. Not surprisingly the level of goods and passenger traffic demanded a four-track facility between Chinley North and New Mills South, accounting for this fine array of semaphore signals. The lines to the left are the through route via Disley to Manchester Central, while the track on the right takes trains to Romiley and east Manchester.

Left During the late '50s and '60s Wakefield shed, 25A, was host to a large allocation of 'WD' 2-8-0s; indeed, the class outnumbered all other types by a considerable margin. In this evocative scene of that period, an unidentified locomotive rolls a heavily loaded coal train down the hill past the shed towards Turners Lane, where it would be routed through Wakefield Kirkgate to Healey Mills yard. Enthusiasts of the day will remember the footbridge access to the shed, seen on the right in the middle distance. The bridge and part of the shed still stand today, but the buildings are not currently in use. Note the sister locomotive in the shed yard and on the left the footplate staff coming off duty.

Below A timeless scene at Southampton Central, although the third rail clearly indicates that the days of steam are numbered. A classic pose is adopted by the fireman as he pushes coal forward and waters BR Class '5' No 73117 with a Waterloo–Bournemouth express in January 1967.

A feature of yesterday's railways which has been totally lost in the monotony of the 1990s was the tremendous variety not just in locomotives but in every facet of railway rolling-stock, trackside furniture and architecture. These pictures show the differing styles adopted for water columns at three sheds: *left* Doncaster (Great Northern), *below left* Heaton Mersey (Cheshire Lines Committee) and *above* Mirfield (Lancashire & Yorkshire). Note that the L&Y columns here were not fitted with a rotating boom, and one wonders just how easy it was to turn on those gas lamps at dusk. . .

The driver of BR Standard tank No 80085 was obviously far more interested in the 'Merchant Navy' which was rattling past at high speed with an express for Bournemouth than in the needs of his trusty steed. Although I was quite pleased with this picture taken at Brockenhurst, I was at the time quite peeved that I had missed the express, since the engine was a particularly clean *Nederland Line*. Note the wheel at the head of the water column which returns the boom safely to a position parallel to the line.

3E2

Left When this photograph was taken on a very dull and foggy November day in 1965, steam in the Doncaster area had been virtually eliminated. Gone were the 'Pacifics', the 'V2s' and the 'B1s'; all that remained were a few heavy freight locomotives to deal with trip freights to local collieries. The scene of emptiness and dereliction is relieved by a solitary 'WD' taking water from one of the columns at the south end of the shed.

Below left A picture which epitomises a typical dismal November day in the heart of the West Riding of Yorkshire. In the days when Wakefield Kirkgate was still a station of some importance, and even boasted a cavernous train shed, two of Wakefield's ubiquitous 'WD' 2-8-0s — the right-hand locomotive is No 90482 — wait for signals on 11 November 1963.

Above A Class '5' eases an empty coal train slowly through platform 5 at Cudworth station just 15 months before closure on 1 January 1968. By this date only platforms 1 and 2 remained in use; indeed, even as a very youthful trainspotter I cannot ever recall seeing a passenger train use platforms 4 and 5, although No 3 (the vantage point for this picture) serviced the push–pull service to Barnsley. The signal box, Cudworth Station South, was the last major structure to be demolished following the work of arsonists in 1988.

Left After a pause to change crews, a '9F' makes a supreme effort to restart a Carlisle–Hunslet freight. On the left is an almost deserted Skipton shed.

Our industrial railways were a Cinderella activity for many enthusiasts; indeed, they were totally ignored by the majority. Nevertheless, in the post-war period the number of private systems was almost equalled by the tremendous variety of locomotives at work. Although most were variants of the well-tried and tested 0-4-0 and 0-6-0 tank engines, there were interesting variants ranging from Garratts and Mallets to Sentinel locomotives, all of course turned out in as many liveries as you could think of. I am for ever indebted to my close friend, Ken Plant, for introducing me to this delightful aspect of our hobby, even though it diverted my interests at times from main-line steam.

Left Ifton Colliery was the last active colliery in Shropshire and was located at the end of a 1½-mile branch from the GW main line at Weston Rhyn. It was a small colliery, in the Staffordshire Area of the National Coal Board, and survived into the late 1960s. It was lately served by two charming industrial locomotives; one, an 0-4-0ST named *Hornet* (Peckett Works No 1935 built in 1937) was typical of the products of the Bristol builder except that it had acquired a dropped cab to accommodate a restricted loading gauge at some time in its career. The other, illustrated here, was a standard Hudswell Clarke 0-6-0 side tank (Works No 1587 of 1927) named *Unity*. This was usually used to work trains down to the exchange sidings. The scene belongs totally to the steam age — note the steam-operated colliery winding gear.

Right A murky winter's afternoon in 1965 at Yorkshire Main colliery near Doncaster finds Class 'O4/8' 2-8-0 No 63653 hard at work pushing empty coal wagons past the washer.

Below The decline in the coal-mining industry in recent times has almost paralleled the demise of steam in the '60s. The National Coal Board generated a great deal of traffic for the railways, particularly the Eastern and London Midland Regions. Reid Class 'J36' 0-6-0 No 65319 was latterly allocated to Bathgate shed and was one of the last survivors of its type; it is seen here picking up a train-load of coal at Riddochill Colliery on 3 June 1966. I was recently invited to use this picture as a basis for a 'then and now' presentation, but was dismayed to find that in 1990 not a single trace of the colliery exists — just green open fields!

Left The Eastern Region shed in the Sheffield area was Darnall, a relatively modern and spacious structure built to replace the very cramped facilities which once existed at Neepsend to the west of Sheffield Victoria. In its post-war heyday it was a very busy shed indeed; in 1950, for example, its allocation included 18 'B1', 2 'C13', 10 'J11', 9 'J39', 2 'J50', 3 'J52', 28 'O4', 17 'N4' and 2 'Y3' locomotives, a total of 91 engines, many of which would be on shed at the weekend. Clearly this 1959 picture was taken midweek and is a view of the shed looking east. Locomotives on shed include a 'WD' 2-8-0, an 'O2' 2-8-0, 'B1' No 61316 and an 'N4' 0-6-2T. Other interesting features are the wagons of prime locomotive coal in the foreground, the coaling tower and, beyond that, the Cravens factory which at the time was just one of the many manufacturers turning out diesel multiple units, sounding the death knell of so many steam locomotives.

Below For many enthusiasts the BR system was just a collection of steam sheds to be visited on Sundays. I certainly recall spending many happy days on coach tours to various parts of the country, although I do have one regret in that I never managed to visit any Welsh steam shed west of Cardiff. The variety of sheds and of course their occupants was quite amazing, ranging from Stratford (where I once recorded just over 350 locomotives) to delightful little sub-sheds which were built to house just one or two engines. Such was Middleton Top on the Cromford & High Peak Railway, where a tiny shed could accommodate just one small locomotive. This picture was taken on 30 April 1967, the last day of operations over the line, by which time the shed had long lost its roof. The two locomotives detailed to work the last train were Class 'J94' 0-6-0STs Nos 68006/12 seen here raising steam for the run back to Buxton. Clearly they had been especially groomed for the occasion.

Above The view from the top of the coaling tower of Holbeck depot might not have been in the top hundred for the average tourist but it was a scene of total fascination for a railway enthusiast. This is looking west in June 1965 when the locomotives on shed included a 'B1', three Stanier Class '5s', an '8F', a Stanier 2-6-4T, two 'Jubilees' and an Ivatt Class '4MT' 'Mogul'. Even the green-liveried Class 25 and Class 47 diesels are of interest. In the middle distance is the viaduct carrying the alternative LNWR line from Leeds City to Farnley Junction. It is also of interest to count the number of tall chimneys in the picture — no fewer than 23. Today just four survive.

Right St Margarets shed, 64A, was rather unique in that it comprised two buildings separated by the North British main line. On the north side was a roundhouse, while on the south was a conventional straight shed, the location of this picture. This photograph brings back a very pleasant memory, since while making this exposure I was invited on to the footplate of the 'V2' by the driver. A long conversation resulted in a never-to-be-forgotten trip on the footplate across the Forth Bridge to Dundee.

Left **Holbeck shed has a permanent place in my memory. Leeds was one of my regular spotting haunts in the early '50s and we usually tried to visit the four major Leeds sheds: Copley Hill, Farnley Junction, Holbeck and Neville Hill. Stourton was conveniently forgotten, as it only housed freight locomotives and was some distance out of the city centre. It was indeed rare for us to have an official permit, and many will recall that Holbeck was not the easiest of sheds to 'bunk' since the one official entrance was alongside the shed office. Athletic junior gricers found illegal access to the roundhouse at the back of the shed through one of the broken windows.**

This picture, taken some 15 years later and this time with the foreman's blessing, always reminds me of those distant days. A grimy and travel-stained 'Jubilee' 4-6-0 No 45573 *Newfoundland* is slowly turned on the turntable in preparation to work a freight north to Carlisle. Sadly this is yet another scene which has been lost for ever.

Above **Although many of the more modern turntables were operated by a vacuum connection to the locomotive being turned, most required muscle power in good measure. The job was made that much easier if the engine could be positioned on the table such that the centre of gravity was over the pivot point. Clearly the crew of this '56XX' 0-6-2T at Croes Newydd shed hadn't quite got their sums right on this occasion; I remember a lot of huffing, puffing, the odd swear word and several invitations for me to help rather than taking xxxxxx pictures! Note the fitter in the background inspecting the valve gear of a BR Class '5' 4-6-0.**

Right **My maternal grandmother lived at Billericay, and as a young boy an annual pilgrimage to what was then a relatively remote part of Essex was eagerly anticipated. The most exciting part of the journey was undoubtedly the run from Liverpool Street when a 'B12' or 'B17' usually provided the motive power. In this August 1951 picture, time was evidently found to wander down to the platform end of the London terminus to photograph No 61637 *Thorpe Hall* on the turntable.**

45593

Right In the latter days of BR steam if there was a clean locomotive at work you could be certain that it would be due to the dedication of just a few station staff and keen enthusiasts. To this day I recall a somewhat unpleasant interview with the manager of Mexborough power station after a friend and I had been apprehended cleaning their Hudswell Clarke shunter! In this picture an apparently immaculate Class '5' No 45350 is hard at work at Lower Darwen on the climb to Sough Summit with the 15.00 Colne to Manchester Red Bank vans. The locomotive had a truly 'Jekyll and Hyde' appearance since enthusiasts had cleaned only half of it the night before; the side which would be on the sunny side for the southbound run to Manchester. Note the station platforms through the bridge; today only a single line survives.

Left The last 'Jubilees' in service were allocated to Holbeck and remained in traffic almost to the end of steam because of the enthusiasm of many of the shed fitting staff. Not only were they kept in good mechanical shape, but externally they were also invariably well groomed. One of the batch, *Alberta*, was for a time absolutely immaculate, so much so that it was even rostered for Royal Train duties. One of the regular 'Jubilee' diagrams was the 15.00 Bradford Forster Square–Heysham vans, a popular subject with local railway photographers. On 23 March 1967 the locomotive rostered was No 45593 *Kolhapur*, seen here coasting into Shipley with a motley collection of stock which includes some four-wheeled vehicles.

Below For more years than I care to remember, one of the highlights of any day's photography in the Leeds area was the Heaton–Red Bank empty newspaper train. The consist often extended to more than 20 bogies and was invariably double-headed. Over the years many unusual combinations of locomotives were noted; the most unusual pairing I ever saw, but unfortunately did not photograph, was a 'K1' piloting a 'Britannia' 'Pacific'. Here, on 5 May 1966, the power was provided by a Stanier Class '5' and a 'B1'. The train is pictured against a typical Leeds background on the LNW new line from City to Farnley Junction.

Above 'Jubilee' No 45647 *Sturdee* powers away from the LNW trans-Pennine line at Springwood Junction, Huddersfield, with the SO Bradford–Weymouth on 2 July 1966. This train was unusually routed through Huddersfield, Penistone, Barnsley and Sheffield, presumably in an attempt to optimise the number of passengers using the service. This photograph was taken with my Exakta Varex IIa fitted with an f4 135mm Sonnar lens using TriX film.

Below South of Preston the number of excellent locations were few and far between, and even those that did exist were unknown to me in the early 1960s. This is another picture which was one of a few taken while on a day's motorcycle trip from Barnsley; on this occasion the destination was Southport. If ever a time machine is invented and I am able to return to 14 May 1960, I will forego the delights of the sea-front at Southport in favour of Wigan! 'Royal Scot' No 46104 *Scottish Borderer* speeds north with a down express; the 1/300th second shutter speed of my Voigtlander Vito IIa at least gave a tolerably sharp picture.

Above This is another picture taken while on the annual summer holiday, this time a tour of North Wales by motor cycle in 1956. I seem to recall a particularly wet and unpleasant week; the sun certainly wasn't shining when this picture was taken of 'Royal Scot' No 46128 *The Lovat Scouts* rolling into Rhyl at the head of a train which is presumed to be a Holyhead–Euston express. The leading vehicle is of particular interest, a GWR Siphon G well off its normal territory.

Below By 1968 the variety of steam locomotives in operation had dwindled to just three or four classes, and all were based in the north-west. However, just one 'Britannia' 'Pacific', No 70013 *Oliver Cromwell*, was wisely retained for use on special trains in the run-up to the end of steam. The locomotive was turned out of Crewe shops in 1967 in immaculate BR livery and was maintained in this condition to the end. No 70013 is pictured here at speed south of Preston with an enthusiasts' excursion bound for Southport on 21 July 1968.

Above A brief hour was spent by the lineside south of Retford on a spring Sunday in 1960. The rest of the day was spent far away from a railway on a beach somewhere near Skegness. This picture was the best of three exposures and shows beautifully clean Peppercorn 'Pacific' No 60130 *Kestrel* at speed with a down express. This photograph all too clearly reveals the limitations of my old Voigtlander Vito IIa; the fastest shutter speed of 1/300th second was quite incapable of 'stopping' any train travelling faster than about 40 mph. Certainly the estimated 80 mph of this train had, as they say, 'beaten the camera all ends up'.

Below The reminiscences of any railway photographer are always tinged with regrets of all the subjects he has missed. It is a source of some comfort to me to learn that an elderly photographer friend who has fine pictures of 'Claughtons' bemoans the fact that he missed the Stirling 'Singles' in everyday service. One of my many regrets is that I never had the opportunity to get to know the Waverley route, although I can recall two fine journeys over the line behind an 'A4' and a 'V2'. At the eleventh hour a special traversed the line on 3 September 1966. Class 'V2' No 60836 is pictured hard at work near Stow, the start of a frenzied chase by car which produced two further shots but of a mediocre standard. It took me a long time to learn that in railway photography quantity rarely equates with quality.

Above No 60034 *Lord Faringdon* accelerates away from Larbert with the 13.30 Aberdeen–Glasgow (Buchanan Street) on 31 May 1966.

Below The beautifully proportioned Peppercorn Class 'A1' 'Pacifics' were among the most elegant of the latter-day express passenger engines to run on British Railways. Friends will no doubt accuse me of a certain bias of viewpoint as a self-confessed LNER fan. These fine locomotives enjoyed a very short lifespan and I well remember this locomotive, No 60118 *Archibald Sturrock*, taking to the rails for the first time. How sad it was to see it in such a run-down and dilapidated condition just 16 years later. There can be little doubt that the passengers on this Scottish Tourist Board CTAC special, comprising just three coaches, had a spirited run to Carlisle on 12 June 1965. I hope they appreciated it. Here the train is seen passing Whitehall Junction on the down fast soon after leaving Leeds City station. Note that another train is signalled on the adjacent slow line to Shipley.

LES NIXON

Above left From LNER to GWR, but there is precious little evidence of the famous polished brass in this bucolic branch-line scene. An unidentified pannier tank takes a pick-up freight bound for Wrexham through the woods near Marchwiel in August 1966.

Left In the early '60s there was a regular incursion of Western Region locomotives deep into the heart of Southern territory at Southampton and Bournemouth. They used to work through on trains from the Midlands, taking the now well-trodden route through Oxford, Reading and Basingstoke. When this picture was taken in August 1962, the Somerset & Dorset offered an alternate route to the South Coast resort but few anticipated that it would be closed, lock, stock and barrel, just three years later. The locomotive featured here is a respectably clean 'Modified Hall' No 7912 *Little Linford Hall*. Note the signal box on the left and in the distance Eastleigh station.

Above To mark the end of services through to Birkenhead via the GWR route through Wolverhampton, Shrewsbury and Chester, two special trains were run on 4 March 1967. Both were 'Castle'-hauled, one by No 4079 *Pendennis Castle* and the other by No 7029 *Clun Castle*. Of the two locomotives, 4079 was certainly preferable from a photographic point of view. The double chimneys fitted to the last batch of locomotives rather spoiled the classic lines of these handsome engines. The conventional three-quarter-front angle of a 'Castle' at work is represented here in this study of No 7029 at speed south of Gobowen.

Right Stafford Road was perhaps the 'glamour shed' in Wolverhampton, but Oxley scored in terms of the sheer number of locomotives allocated there. Although a GWR shed, much of its Swindon heritage was lost in its last years with the influx of large numbers of BR Standard and ex-LMS engines. GWR types were certainly in the minority on a Boxing Day visit in 1965, but happily No 6871 *Bourton Grange* was superbly placed for photography. By this date many ex-GWR locomotives were running without name or cabside plates.

Above **Unrebuilt 'West Country' 'Pacific' No 34102 *Lapford* slithers away from Waterloo with the 17.09 to Basingstoke on 16 May 1967. This was one of a sequence of pictures taken after a business trip to town, and was well worth the chore of the last train home from St Pancras with an arrival at Hathersage at 01.30.**

Right and below **Today enthusiasts are used to paying significant sums for the privilege of visiting BR motive power depots. In the days of steam, shed permits were free, but were not usually available to individuals or to small groups — that is except on the Southern Region. A more tolerant attitude was prevalent there and one of my treasured items of memorabilia is this permit. It was issued for the use of just two people and the only restriction was that we had to show evidence that we had travelled to the location by train! This was, however, hardly a problem when one realises the delights of rail travel at the time. During this tour of the south in the summer of 1953 I made my first visit to Eastleigh Works where, greeting me by the entrance, I found beautifully turned out 'King Arthur' No 30788 *Sir Ure of the Mount*. The picture was taken with my Box Brownie using outdated Selochrome black and white film.**

THE RAILWAY EXECUTIVE (1387 V/MP 1)
SOUTHERN REGION

Reference HO/V/ S
Mr. T. A. Nixon,
76, Spring Street,
BARNSLEY.

MOTIVE POWER SUPERINTENDENT,
WATERLOO STATION, S.E. 1.
2.7. 19 53

DEAR SIR,

In accordance with your request, I have been pleased to arrange for your visit to the undermentioned Motive Power Depot on the date shown below.

Visits should be concluded by 5.0 p.m., unless a later time is specially sanctioned.

This permission is given subject to the presentation, immediately on your arrival at the Motive Power Depot, of this permit together with the return half of Southern Region railway ticket (as indicated below) for each person covered by the permit, it being understood that no person under 16 years of age can visit a Motive Power Depot unless accompanied by an adult.

~~Each visitor must also produce his National Registration Identity Card as proof of British nationality.~~

Photographs may be taken for private collection only.

No luggage (except cameras) must be brought on Motive Power Shed premises.

Motive Power Depot to be visited	Date	Number of persons	Rail tickets to be presented
Feltham	7.8.53	AMENDED TWO ~~ONE~~	YES

Acceptance of this permission will constitute an agreement by or on behalf of each visitor that he/~~she/they~~ will (jointly and severally) be responsible for and release and indemnify the Railway Executive and the British Transport Commission and any other body or person owning working or using the said premises and their servants and agents and any other person whomsoever, occupying being upon or using such premises from and against all actions, claims, losses, costs and expenses by reason of any personal injury (whether fatal or otherwise) delay, or detention, or loss of or damage to property, however caused (whether by neglect or otherwise) and by whomsoever brought, made or suffered occurring in consequence of or in connection with the granting of such privilege.

The permit is not transferable and must be given up before leaving the Shed premises.

Yours faithfully,

For T. E. CHRIMES

Above A busy scene at Ryde Pier Head on 23 April 1966. At the time the Isle of Wight Class 'O2' 0-4-4 tanks were the last steam locomotives of this wheel arrangement still in British Railways service. The engine approaching is No 31 *Chale*, while sister locomotive No 27 *Merstone* waits for the right away; the only train service operating on the island by this date was the local to Shanklin. The watering facility at the end of the platform looks decidedly Heath Robinson, and was clearly a functional and no doubt cheap replacement for an aesthetically more pleasing structure.

Below Semaphore signals were still very much in evidence when this picture of the up 'Bournemouth Belle' was taken at Basingstoke on 23 August 1966. The locomotive is 'Merchant Navy' No 35030 *Elder Dempster Lines*, the last engine of the class. Just visible on the right is a then relatively new Crompton diesel-electric just moving off shed. Note the vintage Pullman stock.

Right In the eyes of the public, railway photography is often thought to be quite straightforward; I have often heard the view proferred that all you have to do is make sure you have a film in the camera and turn up by the lineside. Nothing could be further than the truth; each picture requires very careful thought with regard to composition, exposure, weather conditions and so on. Luck, however, can still make the difference between a competent and carefully thought out shot and one where just about everything is right. When I pressed the shutter of the camera for this picture of Class '5' No 45220 passing Chinley North Junction with a Manchester Central–Sheffield local passenger train in April 1964, I just hoped that I would choose the right moment. For once I did! Note how the rear coach of the train just clears the telegraph pole, the smokebox of the locomotive is just separated from another telegraph pole and, perhaps most fortunate of all, the steam from the safety valve and chimney just misses obscuring part of the signal.

Left Cudworth was the nearest main line to my home town of Barnsley and I recall many, many hours spent on the station, often having travelled the 4 miles on the 'Cud'oth Flyer', a two-coach push/pull service operated by a Midland 0-4-4T. In those days it was a busy place indeed; there seemed to be only minute intervals between the continuous procession of trains. Alas, only a few quality pictures of that period are in my collection, but this scene to the south of the station brings back happy memories. 'Jubilee' No 45562 *Alberta*, at speed with a northbound express, negotiates the complex junction (the line to Stairfoot and Wath can be seen on the right) with an express for Leeds. Today not a trace of the station survives — indeed, the only railway interest now is a pair of lines to nearby Grimethorpe Colliery.

Below Guiseley Junction, Shipley, where the Ilkley line diverges from the Midland Leeds to Carlisle main line, was once graced by a truly splendid array of semaphore signals. Although a delight to the photographer, they were of course necessary because of the then four-track status of the main line. '9F' No 92166 with a freight bound for Carlisle still has steam on as it passes the junction, although it will have slowed to 25 mph for the approaching tight curve round the north side of Shipley triangle.

For me night photography has always been a fascinating aspect of railway photography, probably, I admit, because almost everything is under the control of the photographer. The subject is usually static and the normal nocturnal lighting available at the location can be augmented by fill-in flash. On at least one occasion I have parked a car with the headlamps on to provide additional illumination. Yet another attraction is, of course, the opportunity to make more than one exposure so that if one isn't sure of the correct value (and it can be very difficult to judge this), one can vary it for each shot and at the end of the day select the best of the batch. A sturdy tripod is a must, particularly for photography on windy nights.

Left Stations are usually the easiest places for night photography and more often than not you can get excellent results without the use of flash. This picture of Bulleid 'West Country' *Blackmore Vale*, now preserved on the Bluebell Railway, is one of my favourites. Waterloo has always been a well-lit station for night photography and long exposures were rarely required. This photograph was made on 35mm FP3 film and according to my notes is one of three exposures; 1 minute at f5.6, f8 and f11. Twenty-four years on I am not certain which exposure belongs to which negative! No 34023 is preparing to depart with the 9.25 pm to Bournemouth on 11 September 1966. Note the flats in the distance, a prime location for panoramic views of the terminus, used by many railway photographers in the 1960s. The picture on page 123 of the stock of the 'Bournemouth Belle' was taken from the top balcony.

Left Edgeley shed, Stockport, was ideally placed for night photography, particularly if you kept an eye on the winter evening fixtures of Stockport County football club. The ground of the club was alongside the shed and its floodlights gave superb free lighting for the locomotives in the shed yard. In the 1960s Friday evenings were often a prime time for the tripod brigade; this picture was taken on 15 February 1966.

Above By comparison, Tebay shed after dark was a dull and dismal place; this picture is the result of a 5-minute exposure at f5.6 with no fewer than six fill-in flash bursts from several angles at a distance of around 25 feet. Standard Class '4MT' 4-6-0 No 75039 waits its next turn of duty as one of the Shap bankers at 11.30 pm on a September night in 1966.

Right This station picture is now well and truly part of history. This was the late evening scene at Buchanan Street, Glasgow, in early September 1965, just over a year before it was closed for good on 11 November 1966. It was a particularly memorable occasion for me since this photograph was taken 10 minutes before being welcomed aboard the footplate of Class 'A2' 4-6-2 *Blue Peter* for a never-to-be-forgotten trip to Stirling. This engine is the only one of its class to survive and at the time of writing its return to main-line service 25 years after withdrawal is eagerly anticipated.

DVP 110C

Left On a hot sunny day a clutch of New Forest ponies take shelter under the railway bridge at Battramsley as BR Standard 2-6-4T No 80085 heads a three-coach local towards Brockenhurst from Lymington on 26 August 1966. At the time I was rather concerned by the last-minute appearance of the Land Rover, but in the event it rather adds an extra dimension to the rural scene.

Middle left Towards the end of steam traction in the West Riding of Yorkshire, expresses were often divided at Wakefield Westgate. The diesel locomotive would take the front portion on to Leeds while steam was attached to the rear two or three bogies to form the through service to Bradford Exchange. A variety of locomotives could be found on these duties, but the more usual performers were 'B1s', Class '5s', Ivatt Class '4' 2-6-0s, Fairburn/Stanier 2-6-4Ts and 'Jubilees'. On 17 March 1966 one of the tank locomotives, No 42055, was photographed accelerating away from Westgate at Wrenthorpe Junction. The lines to the right were the former GN metals to Dewsbury and Batley.

Bottom left Seaton viaduct to the south of Ashington was a popular location for railway photography. Even though this picture was taken 25 years ago, I remember my worries as to whether all of the train would be recorded in the photograph. I wasn't sure whether I had been lucky until I developed the film, but as usual the angle of view of the camera was rather more than I had anticipated. A North Blyth Class 'J27' heads south with a rake of 29 wagons and a brake-van on a dismal August day in 1965.

Right A tranquil scene at Swanage in the summer of 1967. Ivatt Class '2' 2-6-2T No 41312 patiently waits for the right away with an afternoon train for Wareham on the main line. Although services have returned to the town under the aegis of the latter-day Swanage Railway, the terminus unfortunately doesn't look quite as attractive as this. Of particular interest here are the two delightful platform seats and the gas lamps appended to relatively modern Southern Railway concrete lamp posts. The delightful single-road engine shed and turntable were located on the right just beyond the bridge. It survives to this day.

Above left Part of the old Cambrian line from Wrexham Central through to Ellesmere survived to the end of steam in the area. Alas, I was never able to photograph the delightful '14XX' tanks which once worked passenger services over this line, but I recall several visits to the area to photograph the trip freights to various works at the northern end of the line. Here 0-6-0PT No 3709, bereft of its cabside number plate, crosses the delightful viaduct near Marchwiel at walking pace in August 1966.

Left The splendid viaduct over Dukes Drive, Buxton, is crossed by an unidentified Class '8F' *en route* to the ICI works at Hindlow with a string of empty wagons. This delightful 4-mile stretch of line is the sole surviving remnant of the former LNW line to Ashbourne; and anyone who has walked over the trackbed of the remainder of the line, known as the Tissington Trail, will have been impressed by the beauty of the scenery and the photographic locations. Sadly I moved into the Peak District 18 months after the line was closed.

Above One of the many steam-hauled excursions which were run on the penultimate weekend of steam traction on British Rail was 1Z79, a Stephenson Locomotive Society excursion from London to Manchester, Huddersfield, Rose Grove and Blackburn. The train, hauled by Class '5s' Nos 44874 and 45017, is pictured making the ascent to Copy Pit as it crosses Cornholme viaduct, Todmorden, on 4 August 1968.

Above Class 'J37' No 64576 brings a desolate scene at Brechin momentarily to life as it rolls in with the daily pick-up goods from Montrose. The branch lost its passenger service from Bridge of Dun and Forfar on 4 August 1952. As can be seen, by 1966 much of the extensive goods yard was being used to temporarily store redundant Conflat A wagons complete with BD 4-ton containers, the forerunners of today's Freightliners. Sadly at this time the proliferation of white-painted smokebox fittings became quite common in Scotland; I for one thought it detracted, rather than enhanced, the looks of a locomotive.

Middle left On the Midland it was the Johnson Class '3F' 0-6-0s which were for many years the locomotives employed on medium-weight freight duties, although they were occasionally pressed into passenger service. No 43181 was photographed in May 1960 taking water from the column located at the north end of platforms 1 and 2 at Sheffield Midland. In days gone by the lines between those that served the platforms were used to temporarily loop northbound freight traffic; today they are normally used to accommodate nothing more exciting than DMUs.

Left The Class 'J39' was intended to be the maid of all work of the LNER but they were probably one of the least successful locomotives to be designed by Sir Nigel Gresley. They were to be found throughout the LNER system although they were somewhat rarer north of the Border. No 64828, then allocated to Colwick shed, 38A, clatters past Radcliffe on Trent in April 1959. Note the GN somersault signals and the signal box.

Above Class 'J38' 0-6-0s were essentially a small-wheeled version of the 'J39'; they were fitted with 4 ft 8 in driving wheels, compared with 5 ft 2 in. Virtually the whole class worked from Fife depots, and No 65921 was a Thornton Junction (62A) locomotive when this picture was taken in September 1965. The location is perhaps one of the most popular in the whole of Scotland — the view looking north to the Forth railway bridge from the footbridge of Dalmeny station. Note the delightful gas lamps.

Below Bathgate shed in the Scottish Lowlands was the last refuge of the LNER Class 'J36' 0-6-0s. No 65319 was built in 1889 by the North British Railway and when this photograph was taken it had already given 77 years of reliable service. Here it is very much on its home territory as it shunts the works of, appropriately, the North British Foundry at Bathgate on 31 May 1966. Fortunately, one of Bathgate's locomotives, No 65345 *Maude*, was saved for preservation by the Scottish Railway Preservation Society and is normally to be found at Bo'ness.

Above As previously mentioned, the last active 'Jubilees' were based at Holbeck and their extended life was a direct result of the enthusiasm of a small band of fitters. By 1966 there were more than enough spare Class '5s' to take over the duties of the 'Jubilees' which, by virtue of their three-cylinder configuration, were more difficult to maintain; but not only were the survivors kept in good mechanical condition, they were also often kept spick and span externally. The cleanliness of No 45647 *Sturdee* certainly made for a good picture when it was photographed struggling manfully with a long freight, the 10.40 Hunslet–Carnforth goods, up the gradient through Calverley and Rodley on 11 March 1966. As can be seen, the four-track main line was still in situ at this time, but only 12 months after the picture was taken the two tracks nearest the camera were lifted.

Left The 'Britannia' 'Pacifics' were never regular visitors to Doncaster in the early days of their life, but one train which could produce one of the East Anglian-based locomotives was the daily train from Norwich to Doncaster. The usual power was one of March's 'B17s' (usually No 61641 *Gayton Hall*), but in May 1959 No 70035 *Rudyard Kipling* was a somewhat unusual visitor. In the 1950s this was the only 'Britannia' allocated to March, 31B, although by 1962 the number of engines had increased to 12. Like many of the class, No 70035 finished its working life at Carlisle Kingmoor, being withdrawn in December 1967. In this photograph the driver casts an anxious backward glance down the platform as the train starts its return journey. Note the group of enthusiasts, young and old, at the extreme left.

Above The outside steam-pipes of the latter-day Class 'V2' 2-6-2s gave them a front end appearance which was not dissimilar to their Class 'A3' stablemates. The modification improved the looks of these fine engines, giving them a more balanced appearance. No 60886 was so modified and was turned out to work an enthusiasts' special on 13 November 1965, seen making a vigorous departure from Wakefield Kirkgate.

Below The New Forest was a popular family area for railway photography; a pleasant day out could be had by all while I was busy with a camera by the lineside. Perhaps the locations didn't have quite the excitement or the grandeur of parts of the north, but at least this part of the country managed to hang on to steam long after the rest of the south had switched to diesels. One of the ubiquitous Bulleid 'Pacifics', No 35014 *Nederland Line*, is seen here at speed near Sway with a down express for Bournemouth. Note the third rail which clearly dates the picture as the summer of 1967.

Above The weekend of 15-16 January 1966 was a particularly cold one and I decided to make a special journey to the south to record the repeat run of the 'S15 Commemorative Rail Tour'. The tour included several branches in Hampshire, and one line traversed was the now well-known preserved Mid-Hants Railway between Alton and Alresford. At the time this picture was taken, the line was complete through to Winchester and was often used as a diversionary route when the main line to Southampton was closed for engineering work. In arctic weather, Class 'N' No 31639 and 'S15' No 30837 charge up the bank from Alton to Medstead. Little did I realise at the time that in less than 25 years I would be able to return to the same spot to photograph an 'S15' at work once more!

Below In dismal light and freezing conditions a grimy Class '5' No 45114 accelerates away from Oxford with a Bournemouth–Midlands relief express in January 1966. Two points are of particular note in this picture. Just visible on the right is Oxford shed with a North British Type 2 diesel standing in the yard, while to the left of the Class '5' is a pair of unusual upper quadrant semaphore signals on a standard GW post.

Above One of the questionable delights of living in the Peak District is that each winter a period of snow is more or less guaranteed. The line over Peak Forest, which reaches an altitude of almost 1,000 feet, could often be under 6 inches of snow while nearby Manchester or Sheffield would have none! Such was the situation when this picture was taken in February 1966. In the Hope Valley there was just a hint of snow but at Chinley North Junction it was a different story; a biting wind tugs at the exhaust of '8F' No 48532 as it picks its way through the snow with a Gowhole–Buxton freight.

Below Many enthusiasts experienced withdrawal symptoms following the formal final end of steam on British Rail on 11 August 1968. Indeed, I recall a half promise to my wife on that day that henceforth 'husband' would be leading a more normal life — in the event a promise unfulfilled to this day! Steam photographers, at home at least, had to be satisfied with the few preserved lines which were operational at the time and the various industrial locations still using steam traction. The best compromise was perhaps those centres where the power was ex-BR locomotives — in the north at least, such locations as the NCB's British Oak disposal point, Wakefield, and Williamthorpe Colliery near Chesterfield took the place of Ais Gill and Shap. At the latter the locomotives regularly employed on traffic to the BR sidings on the main line at Hasland were 'Jinty' 0-6-0Ts Nos 47289, 47383 and 47629, along with ex-Cromford & High Peak Class 'J94' No 68012. In a seasonal flurry of spring snow, No 47289 is seen at the colliery on 21 April 1967.

Right The painted shed plate on the smokebox of No 92234 would suggest it was allocated to Birkenhead when this photograph was taken on 23 March 1967. My notebook indicates that the load of the Barrow–Monkton coal empties on that day was 43 wagons and a brake-van, but it seems that the '9F' was well on top of the job. The train is passing Apperley Bridge and Rawdon station on the up fast; the signal box was switched out and, indeed, was demolished soon after this picture was taken.

Left Of all the British Railways Standard locomotives, my own personal favourite is undoubtedly the '9F' 2-10-0, a machine which managed to combine a powerful Machiavellian image with aesthetic appeal. They were undoubtedly fine engines and they acquited themselves with honour on duties ranging from express passenger work on the Somerset & Dorset to the Long Meg anhydrite hauls over the Settle & Carlisle. Carlisle was the destination of this unidentified '9F' when photographed near Steeton with a very mixed freight from Hunslet in March 1965. This was a typical spring day where the weather alternated between bright sunshine and pouring rain. For once I was lucky in that the train was beautifully lit by the sun whereas the foreground was in total shadow. Fortunately I had the camera set at 'full sun'.

Below Apart from the demolition of the locomotive shed, the railway scene at Hellifield has changed little over the last 25 years, although the station today is in a very dilapidated condition. One photographic technique we used to employ on occasions was to photograph a Carlisle-bound freight here and then follow it by car all the way to Ribblehead. Follow rather than chase was indeed the appropriate word, for 15 mph would be quite commonplace on the steeper parts of the climb. '8F' No 48111 is pictured leaving Hellifield with a Brewery Sidings–Carlisle freight on 1 May 1967; my notebook records three more pictures before the train reached Helwith Bridge.

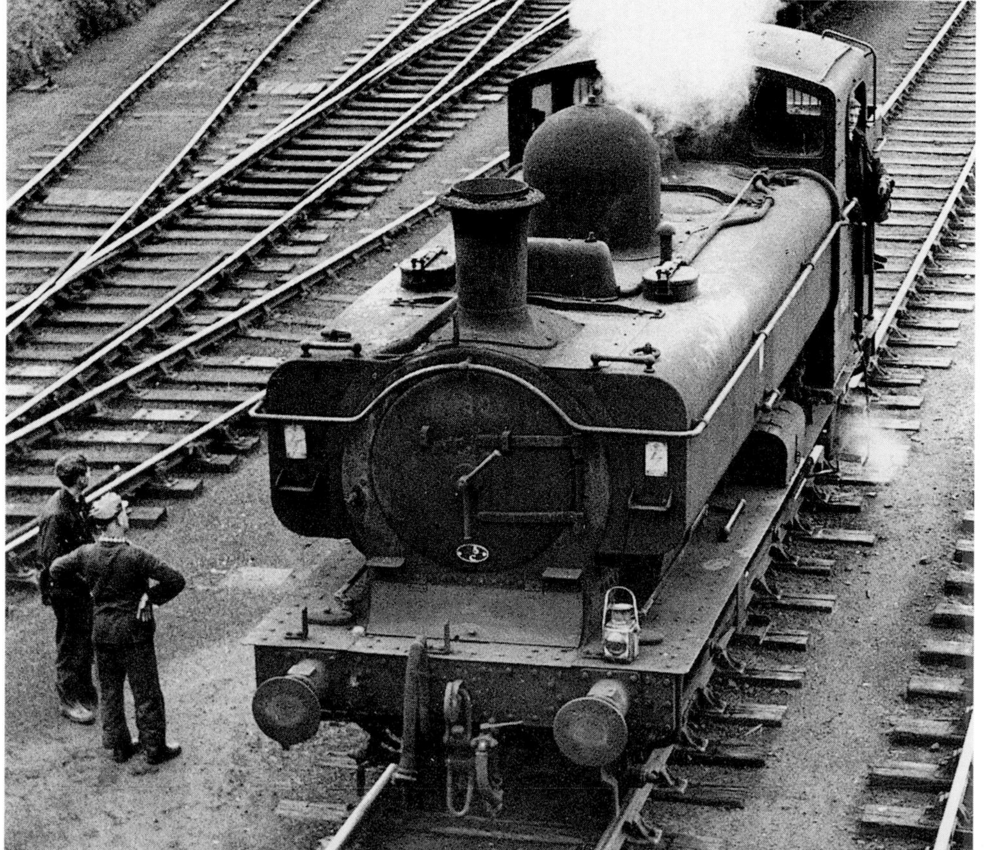

Above **An unusual overhead view of one of the Isle of Wight Class 'O2' tanks while it pauses for business at Ryde St Johns with a passenger train bound for Pier Head. It is often said that it is the smell of the steam engine which makes it so attractive, that 'difficult to describe' aroma resulting from a mix of lubricating oil, burning coal and steam. All the ingredients were here to enjoy that experience to the full.**

Left **The classic lines of the ubiquitous GWR pannier tank are delightfully evident in this study of No 9630 taking a pause between shunting duties at Croes Newydd, Wrexham, in July 1966. By this date many BR locomotives were looking decidedly unkempt and were rarely cleaned. Note here the absence of the familiar GWR cabside number plate and the BR smokebox plate. The driver and shunter (how did they manage in those days without high visibility vests?) are apparently deep in conversation, perhaps discussing the best way to tackle the next shunting movement.**

Above The Vale of Rheidol narrow gauge line was the last outpost of steam on British Rail. Technically steam traction on BR did not formally end on 11 August 1968 since the Rheidol line soldiered on in BR ownership until 1989, when it was sold lock, stock and barrel to the Brecon Mountain Railway. This photograph was taken at the water tank at Devils Bridge in August 1969; the locomotive is 2-6-2T No 7 *Owain Glyndwr*.

Right The station pilots at Sheffield Midland were many and varied in the post-war years. For a long time Midland 0-4-4 and 'Jinty' 0-6-0 tanks were the usual locomotives, but these were eventually replaced by the more modern Ivatt Class '2' 2-6-2TS. In the latter years of steam virtually any small engine which could turn a wheel was used. Ivatt 'Mogul' No 43109 was one of the pilots in April 1965 and is seen here in the deep cutting to the north of the station. Smoke and steam used to hang in this cutting, which includes a number of overbridges and short tunnels, and it was rare indeed to be able to get a clear view for photographs. My notebook indicates that the light for this picture was quite abysmal; an exposure of 1/125th second at f4.5 on TriX film.

Left **The very end of the line for Class 'S15' No 30496 at Eastleigh in August 1963 as the cutting gang get to work to reduce it to scrap metal for razor blades. Surprisingly the locomotive must have been moved into the works under its own steam, since it still has its connecting rods in situ. Note the dome cover by the bottom of the ladder and the recently removed buffer. This engine was the first of Urie's 1920 design for the LSWR and was a development of the Class 'N15' 'King Arthur' for mixed traffic work.**

Above right **A sad scene at Thomas Ward's scrapyard at Beighton near Killamarsh. No fewer than three of the sizeable team then employed on cutting-up duties can be seen at work dismembering an unidentified Class '5' and BR Standard No 73036. It would seem that the 'modus operandi' was first the removal of the buffer beams then the central portion of the boiler shell. The lines in the foreground are the former GC main line south to Nottingham.**

Middle right **Happier times at Eastleigh Works in August 1963. The busy boiler shop was perhaps the least agreeable place to visit — the noise was quite unbearable, particularly if riveting work was in full swing. Prominent in the foreground is a repaired boiler from or destined for 'Merchant Navy' No 35019** ***French Line CGT*** **In my spotting days debates would rage as to whether seeing the boiler was enough to claim a 'cop'; the general consensus I seem to recall was that it didn't count unless you saw the frame of the engine.**

Right **A moment of chaos at Hellifield when 'Britannia'** ***John Bunyan*****, looped at the head of a down freight, ran out of brakes and track and proceeded to make an excellent imitation of a snowplough. The locomotive was well and truly derailed resulting in only limited clearance on the down main line. '9F' No 92205 is pictured passing the stranded Kingmoor engine at a snail's pace with a freight bound for Carlisle. Note the long-demolished Hellifield North Junction signal box.**

Above Debate continues to this day on the looks of the Hughes 'Crab' 2-6-0s. On balance I found them rather attractive locomotives; certainly a design which was distinctly different. Whatever your aesthetic point of view, they were certainly successful, equally at home on passenger and freight duties. Indeed, even quite late in their life they were frequently pressed into express passenger service on busy summer Saturdays. Their last strongholds were Ayrshire and, appropriately, Lancashire. The class was synonymous with the latter county and at one time in 1950 no fewer than 102 of the total of 245 engines were allocated to Lancashire sheds. In 1966 No 42727 was one of a small number of survivors allocated to Birkenhead shed, the location of this photograph. In the company of 'Jinty' 0-6-0T No 47659 and Class '5' No 45139 it is about to be coaled after working trip freights to Cadbury's chocolate factory at Moreton on the Wirral.

Below After a day's work on the Brechin branch, Class 'J37' 0-6-0 No 64577 simmers in the afternoon sunshine at Montrose in June 1966. Note the substantial two-road wooden engine shed and the coaling stage. Today the site is occupied by a large supermarket.

Above Pending decisions on their ultimate fate, a large number of redundant tank locomotives were dumped in sidings within the Canklow (Sheffield) shed complex in 1966. The elimination of steam from the nearby works of Stanton & Staveley accounts for many of the locomotives seen in this forlorn line-up, which includes examples of Deeley 0-4-0ST, Kitson 0-4-0ST, and 'Jinty' 0-6-0T. All were eventually scrapped with the exception of the locomotive nearest the camera, half-cab No 41708, which at the time of writing is to be found on the Swanage Railway in Dorset.

Below Retford once boasted two locomotive sheds; the GN was located to the west of the main line close to the station, while the GC depot was to the south of the east-to-west Worksop–Gainsborough line and approximately 3/4 mile to the east of the famous diamond crossing. The scene here is the GN shed on a sunny Sunday afternoon in the spring of 1965. One of the 'WD' 2-8-0s was being steamed ready for work early on Monday morning, but at least one of the other two would seem to be a candidate for the scrapyard judging by the absence of connecting rods.

60034

Right Generations of railway photographers have appreciated the superb scenic backdrop of the railway at Chinley North Junction. It was an open spot with plenty of traffic, being the dividing point of the Midland routes through the Hope Valley and the main line to Derby. Add to this a gradient of 1 in 90 and it was obvious that here were all the ingredients for first class railway pictures. The favoured time of day was afternoon when, with the sun shining and a westerly wind, it was possible to show the Pennine hills to best effect. All the elements certainly came together for me on this occasion when I was more than pleased to press the shutter to record the passing of an '8F' with a freight for Derby.

Left Aberdeen was a city which was to retain its complex mechanical signalling well into the diesel era. However, this photograph was taken in 1965 when the surviving Gresley 'A4s' were in the final chapter of their life, working the 3-hour expresses to Glasgow. No 60034 *Lord Faringdon* addresses itself to the steep 1 in 96 climb to Ferryhill with the 13.30 to Glasgow Buchanan Street in September 1966. Although it was difficult to gain official lineside access here, it was a location where spectacular smoke effects were more or less guaranteed. Ironically I was to return to the same location 13 years later, in the era of preserved main-line steam, to photograph a similar departure behind preserved 'A4' No 60009 *Union of South Africa*. Surprisingly, apart from enthusiasts hanging out of almost every window, the photograph was almost identical. Occurrences like this are, however, the exception; most photographs of today's outings of preserved steam bear little resemblance to the real thing.

Below The last steam-hauled passenger train through the Peak District ran on 27 April 1967 when Class '5s' Nos 44781 and 45046 headed an enthusiasts' special which took the train over the LNW line from Stockport to Buxton via Whaley Bridge and back to Lancashire via Ashwood Dale, Peak Forest and Chinley. The pair are pictured storming away from Chinley on the down fast watched by a surprisingly small group of onlookers.

Many photographers deign not to take pictures of trains when the sun isn't shining. Indeed, until almost the end of steam on BR most photographers were not active in the winter months. Certainly chill winter days make it hard work to produce exceptional pictures, but they do lend themselves to atmospheric studies in steam, and such pictures are a pleasing foil to the more traditional sunny three-quarter-front studies taken in high summer. The industrial cities particularly lend themselves to this treatment, and steam was as much a part of the scene as were gas lamps, cobblestones and terraced houses.

Above and left Class '5' No 44913 moves a heavy freight out of Hunslet, Leeds, towards Holbeck on a murky November day in 1965. I did regret that the foreground interest was a modern colour light signal, but eagle eyes will spot the odd gas lamp! *Left* Ten seconds later the 'wind on' shot was equally evocative; the shutter was released at the precise moment the exhaust from the engine was deflected by that offending gantry — it did after all serve one useful photographic purpose!

Above right The locomotives of the steam era probably contributed in no small way to the smogs and fogs so prevalent in my youth. This scene encapsulates my memories of winters years ago; a disagreeable murky atmosphere does its best to beat the photographer at Leeds City station on 4 December 1965 as a brace of 'Jubilees', Nos 45654 *Hood* and 45596 *Bahamas*, struggle manfully to restart an eastbound Railway Correspondence and Travel Society excursion. The intensity of the lights of the shunting signals, seen at the bottom left, would seen to confirm the exposure written in my notebook, 1/125th second at f3.5 on TriX film.

Right Locomotives travelling tender first rarely afforded good photographs, but here was an occasion when even a light engine movement produced a quite evocative image, with the trailing swirling steam beautifully highlighted by the low sun of a very frosty January morning in 1965. The '9F' had just completed shunting the yard at Hathersage in the Hope Valley and was returning light back to Sheffield.

RCTS
45654
1X36

The humble tank engine is perhaps under-represented in this volume, so this vignette of portraits is an attempt to redress the balance.

Above **The GWR '56XX' 0-6-2T locomotives were introduced in 1924 to the design of Collett, and the class was expanded to a total of 200 engines. Most were to be found at work in the Welsh Valleys where they were equally at home on short-haul freight shunting and local passenger duties. No 5676 takes things easy in the roundhouse at Croes Newydd in August 1965.**

Below **The large-wheeled Prairie tanks of the '61XX' series were synonymous with suburban traffic duties out of Paddington. The whole class of 70 locomotives was allocated to Old Oak (81A), Slough (81B), Southall (81C), Reading (81D), Didcot (81E) or Oxford (81F). No 6134, for many years a Didcot engine, had turned its last wheel in revenue-earning service when this photograph was taken at Oxford in January 1966.**

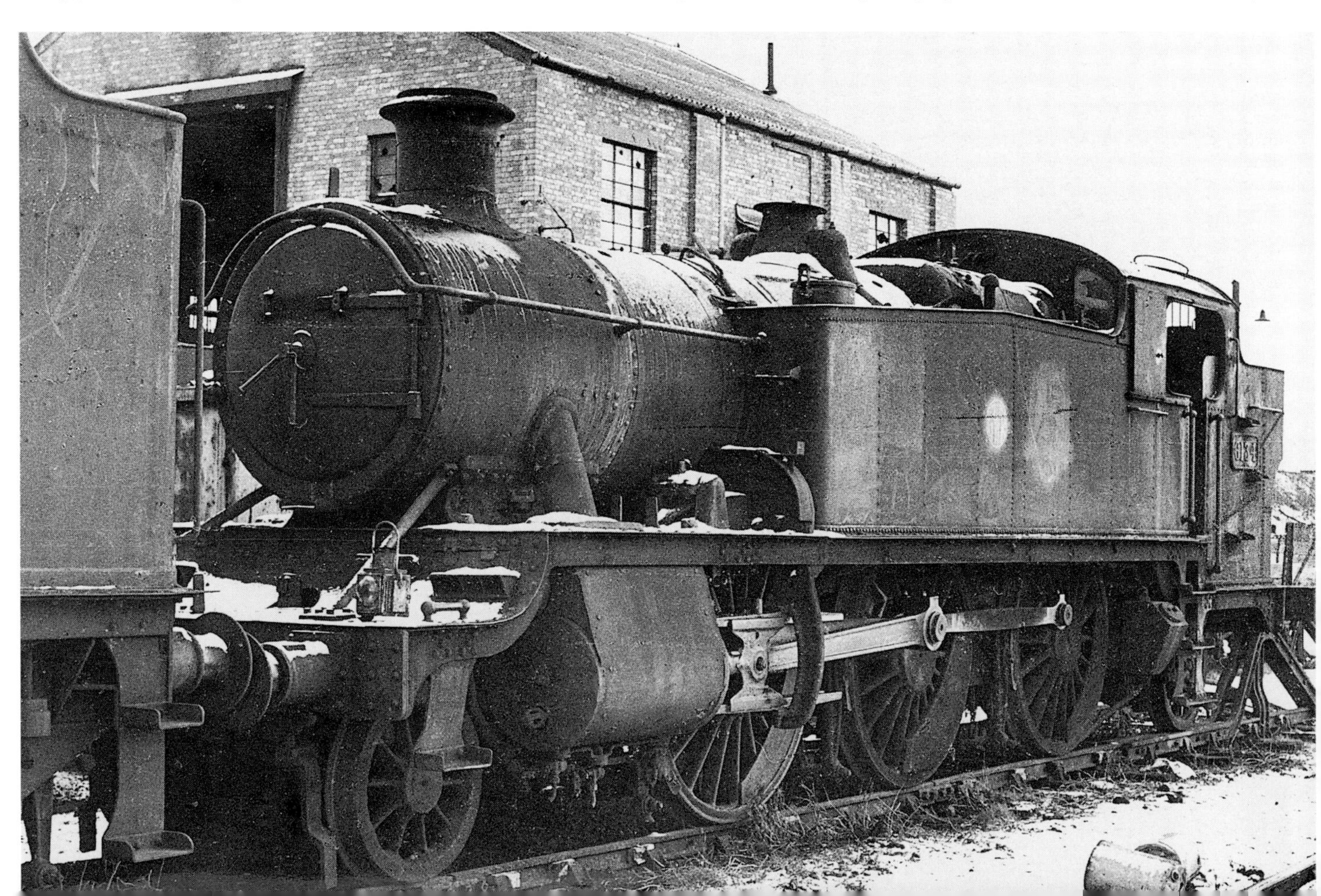

Above The classic lines of the beautifully proportioned Lancashire & Yorkshire 0-6-0ST are nicely portrayed in this study of No 51424 at Mirfield shed. The photograph was taken in 1959 and, judging by the blurred drifting steam, a lengthy exposure was used.

Right Another picture which is now nearly 40 years old. The slightly blurred outline confirms that it is a product of my Box Brownie, but at least the subject is of particular interest. One of the eight Class 'Z' 0-8-0T engines, No 30953, was pictured during shunting movements at Ashford. A number of these powerful locomotives were allocated to Exmouth Junction, Exeter, for banking duties between St Davids and Central.

Below The 'C13' 4-4-2Ts were among the first steam locomotives I ever saw; I am told I used to see them regularly from my pram at Jumble Lane level crossing, Barnsley. They were certainly handsome machines, but I do regret not having seen them with their rather more elegant Robinson chimney. No 67439 stands in the yard at Sheffield Darnall in July 1959.

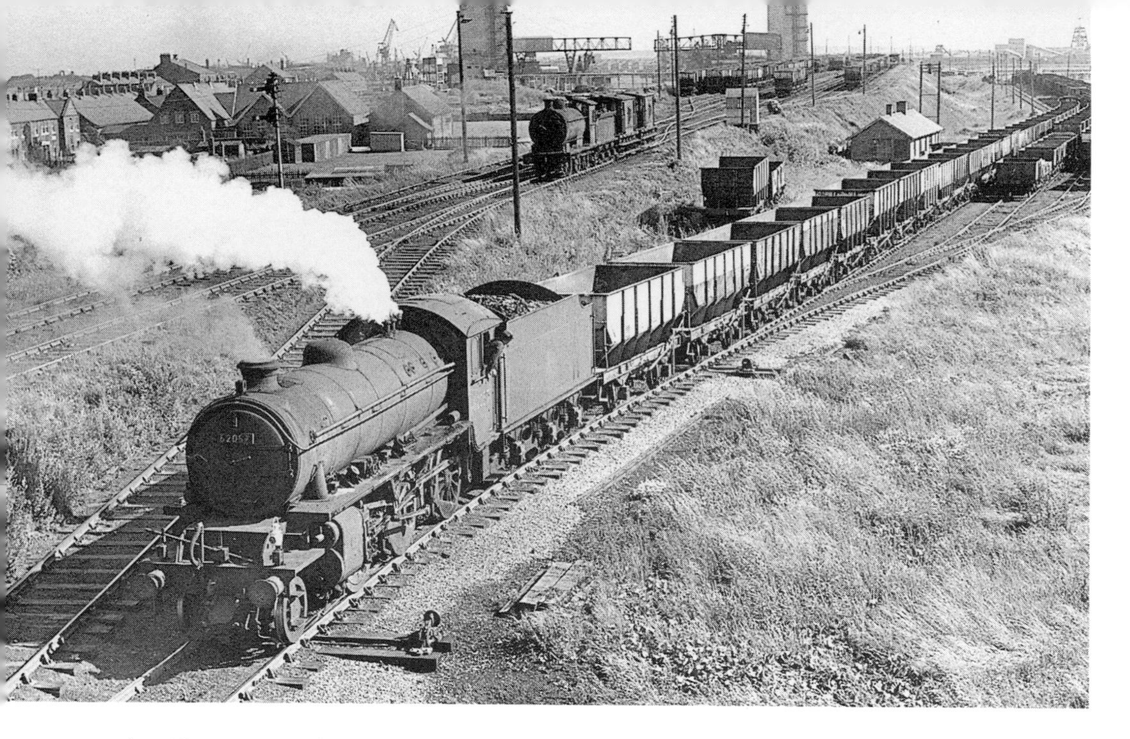

Left In the 1950s, when a substantial tonnage of coal was exported from Blyth in Northumberland, no fewer than 24 'J27s' were allocated to Blyth shed to handle the traffic. In later years the allocation was augmented by a few Ivatt Class '4' and 'K1' 2-6-0s. One of the latter was No 62057, a locomotive which was allocated to Darlington for many years. Here it waits to leave North Blyth with a string of empties for Ashington. Note the shunter's pole on the buffer beam.

Below The Great Northern Railway once had a vast network of lines in the West Riding of Yorkshire but rationalisation in the 1950s and 1960s decimated the system. Ironically in the many cases where duplicate routes linked two towns, it was usually the GN which was closed. One notable exception which survives to this day is of course the line from Bradford Interchange to Leeds. One truncated GN remnant which survived into the 1970s was the line from Shipley (near to the former terminus at Whin Hill) to Idle. The goods yard here was the reason why the branch was retained and it usually generated enough traffic to require three trains per week. On 18 February 1967 Ivatt Class '4' No 43077 was employed on the trip working from Bradford. The train, comprising five coal wagons and a brake-van, is seen climbing away from Guiseley Junction and the Midland main line. Incidentally, the main tourist attraction in the area was the mythical Idle Working Men's Club!

Above **'J94' No 68006 rounds the tight curve at Gotham and crosses one of the many unprotected level crossings which characterised the Cromford & High Peak line. The payload of the daily freight, two old tenders for carrying water to Middleton Top and a brake-van, was typical of the latter days of the line's life. Note the Heath Robinson arrangement on the cabside to protect the crew from the rigours of Pennine winter weather.**

Below **The Leslie branch in Fife was closed to passenger traffic on 4 January 1932 but survived long after this date to serve a distillery and two paper mills. The mill at the end of the branch, Smith & Anderson, will be familiar to many enthusiasts since one of the directors was the well-known railway photographer W.J.V. (Bill) Anderson, who vowed that rail traffic to the mill would survive as long as it was steam-hauled. Here Thornton (62A) 'J38' No 65909 eases out of the mill over weed-covered track with the daily freight on 2 September 1966. True to his word, rail traffic ceased soon after dieselisation.**

42737

Left 4 March 1967 was a delightful spring day, and a day to remember in many respects. It was to be the last occasion that 'Castles' worked the full length of the former GW line from Shrewsbury to Chester and Birkenhead. It was also the last time that steam locomotives were scheduled to haul the 'Cambrian Coast Express'. Inevitably photographers laid plans to photograph each of the trains as many times as possible, but I elected to shoot the last 'CCE' rather than opt for a picture north of Chester. Standard Class '4MT' 4-6-0 No 75021 was the engine detailed to work the down train and is seen here near Wollaston close to the Welsh border. Note the wreath on the smokebox door and an apparently clean locomotive. In truth it was a rather rough and ready job, a far cry from the immaculate 'Manors' which used to work the service in the early '60s. I recently returned to this very spot to photograph today's equivalent of the service, only to find mature 20-foot trees totally obscuring the view.

Below left One of Ayr's 'Crabs', No 42737, is hard at work at the head of a freight of more than 40 wagons passing the station at Hollybush (closed 4 April 1964) on the Dalmellington branch in September 1966. The leaking steam rescued a potentially bland picture, separating the locomotive from the background.

Above One of the last forays of a 'Crab' into Yorkshire took place on 8 October 1965 when No 42942, a Birkenhead locomotive, worked a Locomotive Club of Great Britain special from Liverpool to Goole via the former trans-Pennine Lancashire & Yorkshire main line through the Calder Valley. It is pictured here with steam to spare as it approaches Horbury Junction on the outward leg. Note how diligent cleaning has revealed part of the LMS legend on the tender. The second coach is also of particular interest, being one of only a few of Thompson design still in service at the time. One wonders whether passengers in this vehicle were subjected to a surcharge!

Below Carnforth was one of the last operational BR steam sheds; indeed, it fell to this depot to provide the men and locomotives to work the last steam-hauled freight train. This picture was taken on 25 July 1968, just two weeks before the end, when Carnforth Class '4' No 75048 was caught by the camera at the head of the return working of the daily Carnforth–Ulverston freight. The train is seen approaching Cark and Cartmel station, but what the camera hasn't recorded is the Class 40 diesel-hauled passenger train travelling in the opposite direction which almost eclipsed the steam.

GENTLEMEN
PARCELS
AND LEFT
WAITING ROOM

Right The precise date of this picture is unknown, but it was taken during a visit to Derby Works in either 1953 or 1954. The location was the footbridge connecting the station forecourt area with the Works and I recall poking my camera through the girder latticework to get this picture of Class '5' No 45318 about to leave with a southbound local train. The remainder of the pictures taken that day were rather uninteresting portraits of 'foreign' locomotives, although one features the Lickey banker No 58100. Surprisingly, apart from the disappearance of the signals and the bridge itself, little has changed in this view of the station today.

Above left Fairburn 2-6-4T No 42175 rolls into Bradford Exchange at the foot of the 1 in 50 bank from Laisterdyke with a four-coach local from Leeds. By any standards Exchange station was a splendid structure, built to service both L&Y and GN trains in the early 1870s when the latter extended its tracks into the city centre from Hammerton Street. The magnificent twin 100-foot arched roof of the train shed is behind the photographer. The station was demolished just four years after the end of steam and a much less grandiose replacement built just beyond the bridge.

Left This is a photograph which has been published before but it is a personal favourite and I felt that I just had to include it in this album. It encapsulates so perfectly the steam era of yesteryear, a scene which was enacted every day at thousands of locations throughout the country. His work over, having checked the tickets and escorted the joining passengers, the duty porter, hands in pockets, saunters back to his office as the 17.30 local ex Sheffield leaves Hope for Manchester. No TV aerials, no high-visibility vests, no graffiti, no cars — halcyon days.

Left Perth is perhaps the finest surviving main-line station in Scotland, eclipsing even Edinburgh Waverley. It was also one of the best places to see, in quantity, the last of the steam-hauled express trains in Scotland. Of particular interest were the Aberdeen–Glasgow Buchanan Street expresses which were routed north via the Caledonian route through Cupar Angus and Forfar. No 60019 *Bittern* pauses at the south end of the station with the 13.30 ex Aberdeen; the crew standing by the water column look none too pleased with the prospect of coaxing their mount into a high-speed dash to Glasgow.

Above Few enthusiasts visiting Preston wandered far from the main line, but close by was a particularly interesting railway system, serving the docks of the Port of Preston Authority. The system extended to around 6 miles of track and apart from an Armstrong Whitworth diesel delivered in 1932 was worked exclusively by steam until 1968. The locomotive fleet was relatively modern, comprising seven 0-6-0ST locomotives built by William Bagnall, Stafford, between 1942 and 1948. In this charming dockside scene, *Enterprise* (Works No 2840 of 1946) poses at the head of a string of antique five-plank wagons lettered 'PC' together with their fleet number.

Left Sentinel locomotives were specifically designed for modest shunting duties at minimal cost. They used a small vertical boiler and were chain driven, but in spite of their small size could move quite substantial trains, albeit at very slow speeds. Two classes of Sentinel, the 'Y1' and 'Y3', survived Nationalisation and were allocated to sheds as diverse as Selby, Lowestoft and Wrexham. Several examples saw industrial service, including *St Monans* (Sentinel Works No 9373 of 1947), which in the late 1960s was in regular use at the Newark works of British Gypsum & Co Ltd. The picture was taken on 1 January 1970 just a few months before the locomotive was withdrawn.

Right A stirring scene at Bickershaw Colliery in Lancashire on 15 April 1977. One of the ubiquitous standard Hunslet 0-6-0 saddle tanks, No 5 *Gwyneth*, blasts up the grade from the colliery to the BR exchange sidings. These locomotives were worked to the limit for this steep climb of around 1 mile and were at this time probably the finest spectacle of steam at work in the British Isles.

Above To an enthusiast who grew up with Great Central locomotives, any design from a 'foreign' railway, even one from a company which became an integral part of the LNER in 1923, was regarded with a degree of disdain. Perhaps I should admit to also being brainwashed from an early age by my father who was a GC man through and through. In my very early years I am told that I used to pester him to draw pictures of steam engines, and I now realise that I was peddled with a mix of Class 'J11' 'Pom Poms', 'N5' tanks and GC 'Atlantics'! The GN 0-6-0s I used to think of as very spindly and somewhat fragile-looking machines; indeed, like many GN locomotives they used to sound strangely effeminate too. Times change, however, and I would now love the opportunity to ride again behind a 'J6' as I did on this day in 1959 when I caught a train from Nottingham to Radcliffe on Trent, the location of this photograph. The engine is No 64215 of Colwick (38A) shed. Note the GN builder's plate on the central splasher, an item of railwayana which today would realise the best part of a four-figure sum.

Left This is one of my very earliest railway pictures, taken on a family holiday to Yarmouth in 1951. Even to a 14-year-old spotter, the elegant lines of Holden's 4-4-0s warranted the exposure of a precious frame of film. This is No 62507, one of the Class 'D15' locomotives built at Stratford in 1900, being turned on the turntable at Kings Lynn. It was scrapped the following year. In the background can be glimpsed a GE 'J69' 0-6-0T.

Above Another of my earliest railway pictures, also taken in the summer of 1951, features my favourite LMS class, the unrebuilt 'Patriots'. No 45548 *Lytham St Annes*, the last of the class, was photographed ex-Works glinting in the afternoon sun at Crewe North shed. The camera obviously had a faulty viewing system since many of the pictures I took with it were cursed with the same fault — the loss of part of the extreme right of the picture.

Below The former Great Central Robinson Class 'D10' and 'D11' 4-4-0s were a very familiar part of my youth. Many is the time I have scorned yet another sighting of *Marne* or *Prince of Wales*. I have few photographs of these fine engines but I hope I may be allowed to include just one portrait which will remind me of those distant days. 'D11' No 62669 *Ypres* was looking a little woebegone when this picture was taken at Darnall shed in 1959, for even by this date there was little work for these locomotives and all had gone by the dawn of the next decade.

Left **The view from the top of the coaling tower at Rose Grove towards the end of July 1968, when there was the prospect of less than three weeks of further active steam in the north-west. The rather melancholy scene shows five abandoned '8Fs' and two Class '5s', although there were many more in this condition scattered around the shed yard. Note the presence of at least four other enthusiasts paying their last respects. A view from this point today would give a splendid aerial perspective of the M65 motorway.**

Above **Langwith Junction on Saturday 9 October 1965 is host to a 'WD' 2-8-0, two 'O4/8' 2-8-0s (No 63706 on the right) and '9F' 2-10-0 No 92200; the '9F' was withdrawn from service the week after this picture was taken. Judging by the delapidated roof it would seem that the shed had seen better days. By this date much of its work had been transferred to the new diesel servicing depot at Shirebrook. This too closed in 1991 and facilities were transferred to new premises at Worksop.**

Below **Writhing smoke and steam envelop a couple of Scottish steam stalwarts on Dundee shed in August 1965. 'B1' No 61244** ***Strang Steel*** **was a Scottish locomotive for almost all of its working life, and was one of the more difficult named 'B1s' for enthusiasts south of the Border to see. It eluded me for many years; indeed, this was my first sighting and was probably one of the reaons why I took this particular picture.**

Above One of the undoubted attractions of the steam era was the number of branch lines still in operation. I once had good intentions to visit as many as I could, but in the event it was the lure of the sheer quantity of trains at the major rail centres which often won the day. Thankfully there were exceptions and, if I could turn the clock back, there would have been many more. One such occasion was 2 September 1966 when I decided not to photograph main-line steam in Fife but instead to take a few pictures on the Lathalmond branch. The line diverged from the North British Dunfermline–Kelty route, the connection to Lathalmond being made by a trailing connection at Gask Junction. Class 'J37' No 64611 is seen from the junction shunting the yard of the Royal Naval Storage Depot; the Depot closed to rail traffic on 30 June 1971.

Left Today the former LSWR main line to Southampton is one of the busiest in the country, but how much nicer it was in days gone by when most of the trains were hauled by steam. Even at the eleventh hour of steam, the Bulleid 'Pacifics', in spite of their latter-day run-down condition, were putting in some sparkling performances on this, the last steam-operated line in the south. Standard Class '5' No 73093 was performing admirably on 30 June 1967 when it was caught by the camera near Micheldever with a relief for Bournemouth.

Above Green issues had apparently not been invented in the 1960s! Smoke from dirty steam engines and detergents in the rivers and canals were an everyday sight in many parts of the country. Perhaps this scene isn't one which would be used to promote popular tourism in Wakefield, but I would personally travel some distance for a similar experience in 1991. An unidentified 'WD' 2-8-0 takes an empty coal train eastbound over the Aire & Calder canal near Wakefield Kirkgate in October 1965.

Below 'B1' No 61161 rounds the curve to Wortley West Junction with the three-coach portion of a King's Cross–West Riding express. The park at Copley Hill was a delightful spot for railway photography, close to the steam shed with easy access to the Leeds–Bradford and Leeds–Doncaster main lines.

Left Swinden Limeworks at Cracoe in the heart of the Yorkshire Dales is shunted by BR Class '4' No 75027 on 21 June 1968. By this date Skipton shed had closed and this was the sole surviving steam turn into the area from Rose Grove shed. As late as 1966 the complete branch through to Grassington was open to freight traffic.

Below Middleton Quarry near Wirksworth in Derbyshire, located high in the hills above Cromford, ranked as one of the more inaccessible locations of British Railways. It was served by a branch off the line linking the top of Sheep Pasture and the bottom of Middleton rope-worked inclines near to Steeple House and Wirksworth goods station on the Cromford & High Peak line. A small tank locomotive was allocated to the small shed at the top of Sheep Pasture (a sub-shed of 17D, Rowsley) to work traffic between the two inclines. On 25 July 1965 Class '0F' 0-4-0ST No 47006 eases out of the quarry complex and across the unprotected road under the watchful eye of one of the quarry employees.

Right The lime-burners at Hindlow overlook the yard adjacent to the former Buxton–Ashbourne line. At close on 1,100 feet above sea level, this stretch of railway is the highest in the Peak District, and even today represents a continuing operational problem for British Rail's Buxton staff. A remarkably clean '8F', No 48744, poses for the photographer in the snow in February 1968 before departure for Buxton.

Below right Coal traffic in the North East was associated with the Class 'J27' 0-6-0s and the 'Q6' 0-8-0s, both sturdy North Eastern Railway designs which gave years of yeoman service. Large numbers of 'J27s' were allocated to North and South Blyth sheds in Northumberland, and indeed many spent virtually the whole of their working life in the area. This photograph depicts No 65811 on 10 August 1965 as it storms past Woodhorn Colliery with a loaded coal train from Lynemouth.

48744

Above **The two locomotives which worked the second 'S15 Commemorative Rail Tour'** **(see page 72)** **stand on the reception road at Eastleigh shed on 16 January 1966. On the left is Class 'N' No 31639, and on the right Class 'S15' No 30837. Many years after taking this picture, and after several visits to Eastleigh, I noticed the unusually placed semaphore signal attached to the side of the water tank above the tender of the leading locomotive. To this day I am not certain why it was there; the most popular theory is that it was used as a vision test for engine crew.**

Left **A pleasant warm sunny Saturday afternoon in May 1968 at Bolton sees a couple of remarkably clean Stanier Class '5s', Nos 44947 and 45110, taking their turn to be coaled. Note the numerals '1' and '2' on the coaling tower, indicative that the shed was once a very busy depot. No 45110** ***Biggin Hill*** **was the engine which worked the last steam-hauled BR train out of Liverpool Lime Street on 11 August 1968.**

Above right **Class 'Q6' 0-8-0 No 63387 cautiously approaches the ash disposal pit and coaling tower at Normanton shed. Normanton was one of those fascinating depots with both an ex-LMS and ex-LNER allocation of locomotives, which no doubt prompted friendly rivalry between engine crews in days gone by.**

Right **'V2' No 60832 is pictured under the coaler at York shed on 18 September 1965. Note the diminutive stature of the driver — perhaps an attribute required of Eastern Region crew who were to pass through the corridor of an 'A4' tender!**

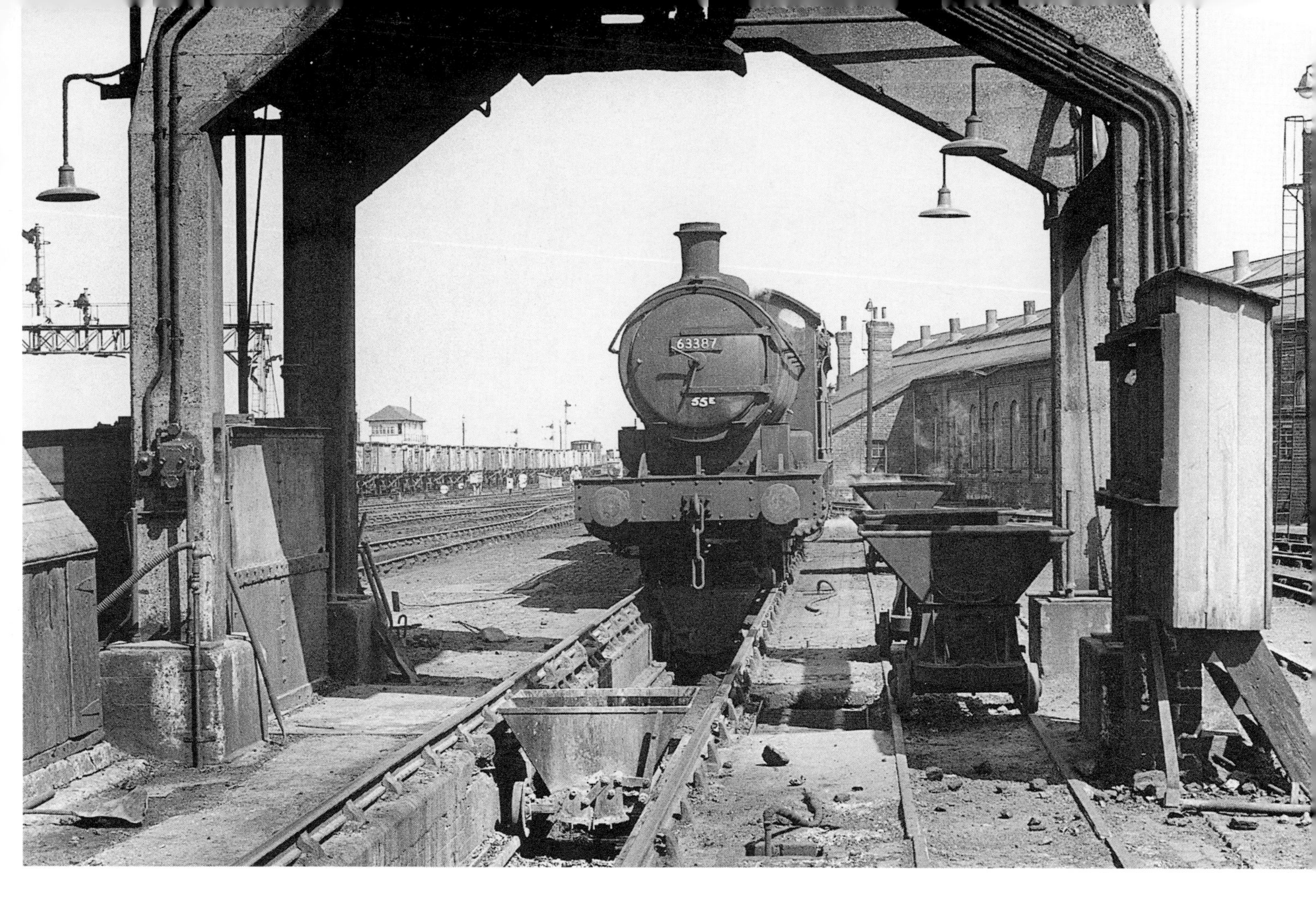
63387
55E

Above **The triangle of lines at Chinley encircle a small church and a cemetery, and my wife, in her more light-hearted moments, tells me that she has reserved a space here for me when I pass on to the hereafter. Apparently she considers it is the only place near to home where I would be able to rest in peace (?) — completely surrounded by trains and excellent locations. Certainly this delightful spot at Chinley South Junction is just half a mile away. '8F' No 48171 is down to walking pace on the 1 in 90 climb to Peak Forest in March 1965. The missing signal arms on the gantry had just been removed; of each trio the missing centre arm was a distant relating to the down slow at Chinley North, while the missing arms on the right once controlled access to the curve to Chinley East Junction and the Hope Valley, a line which was reinstated ten years ago.**

Left **Class '8F' No 48191 approaches Dore West Junction, with a limestone train bound for South Wales. The train is about to take the curve to Dore South, a route regularly used by freight trains to and from Cheshire and Lancashire to avoid the centre of Sheffield. A photographer at this location just 35 years ago could well have been photographing LMS 2-6-0+0-6-2 Garratts!**

Right Gas lamps, semaphore signals, four-wheeled vans and a Stanier Class '5' represent the old order on the West Coast Main Line at Preston in the 1960s. The locomotive is No 44949.

Below Colour light signals were not part of the railway scene when the North Eastern Railway 'Q6s' were introduced in 1913. In this 'ancient and modern' study at Seaton Carew, just south of Hartlepool, No 63445 is looped to allow a DMU to pass, forming a local service to Darlington. Note the strange antics of the guard at the rear of the train.

OXENHOLME No2

Above The signalman at Smallbrook Junction on the outskirts of Ryde in the Isle of Wight offers the token to the crew of Class 'O2' 0-4-4T No 31 *Brading* at the head of a vintage rake of stock bound for Shanklin in August 1965. This operation called for slick operation since the exchange occurred at a speed of 30-35 mph — fast enough I imagine to break an arm if the pick-up wasn't executed properly. The procedure looks fairly straightforward here, but maybe it was a different story on a windy and rainy night in mid-winter.

Left The peace and quiet of Oxenholme is disturbed by Class '5' No 44894 as it wheels a northbound freight through the train shed spanning the Windermere branch line platform on 28 July 1968. The steam age scene, so charmingly evident here, was to disappear under a plethora of 25kV catenary in less than six years. Of particular interest are the gas lamp, the semaphore signals and of course the signalman of Oxenholme No 2 signal box. Some 25 years ago Oxenholme station hit the national headlines when a macabre murder was committed in one of the waiting rooms.

Right Laisterdyke signal box on the GN line to Leeds was 1¾ miles from the centre of Bradford and one of those interesting structures which straddled the running lines. Other examples were once to be found in places such as Hexham, Matlock and Armley near Leeds. Passing the box is grimy Class '5' No 45191 with the Bradford portion of a West Riding to King's Cross express. The lines to the left of the box connected with the L&Y exit from Bradford Exchange at Bowling.

Left A long gruelling climb of 7 miles to Grayrigg and a further 5 miles to Shap summit is ahead of Kingmoor Class '5' No 44727. With a very heavy freight of around 45 vans in tow, it was not surprising that the crew elected to pause at Oxenholme for a banker. A BR Class '4' can be seen buffering up to the rear of the train while the crew of the Class '5' make sure that they start the climb with a full head of steam. Even with a banker, progress was slow and I managed to get further pictures at Low Gill, Greenholme and Shap summit. Oxenholme station, along with the branch to Windermere, can be seen on the right of the picture.

Below A more traditional view of the northern exit from Oxenholme, as '9F' No 92223 picks up speed to have a run at Grayrigg.

Above **A modest 80mm telephoto lens fitted to my trusty Exakta emphasises the delightful hump of the yard situated on the north side of the line at Rose Grove. A remarkably clean Class '8F' 2-8-0 No 48348 (no doubt the result of hard work by enthusiasts the night before) raises steam ready for the arduous climb to Copy Pit summit with almost 50 wagons in tow. By the time the train was halfway up the bank it was down to walking pace, and the sound, I recall, was quite unbelievable.**

Below **The Lune Gorge was a delightful, sheltered valley and, in the days before the M6, a tranquil place to spend a relaxing afternoon (that was when the light was best for photography). At the northern end of the gorge were the troughs at Dillicar which have been the subject of many fine railway photographs; the best, perhaps, when the camera has caught the precise moment when excess water cascades out of the tender. Despite numerous attempts I never had the good fortune to be at the right place at the right time. One of my better shots there was this one of Class '5' No 45312 with a northbound freight on 17 June 1967.**

Whenever steam takes to the main line today it is almost certain that there will be hundreds, if not thousands, of people out by the lineside hoping for a momentary glimpse of nostalgia. Dedicated enthusiasts will climb into their cars and, with a bit of high-speed chasing, hope to photograph the train a second or even a third time. How different this is to days gone by when the laid-back photographer could select his stretch of line and let the trains come to him. As mentioned on the previous page there was no finer spot than the Lune Gorge on a fine summer's day; I seem to recall that the only major problems were whether the sun would shine (at least this aspect hasn't changed over the years!) and, if it did, whether you had enough film with you to photograph everything that came along. One such day was 22 August 1967 when this picture of 'Britannia' No 70011 *Hotspur* on a down freight was taken on the Exakta fitted with an 80mm Biometer lens.

There is little doubt that the Class 'A4' 'Pacifics' were among our best-loved steam locomotives. No 60025 *Falcon* speeds non-stop through Doncaster with a King's Cross–Newcastle express in May 1959. Note the post-war signal box to the right of the picture, now itself replaced by a modern power box. This is another picture which stirs youthful memories of hours spent on Doncaster station or St James Bridge, when the appearance of an 'A4' would be greeted by euphoric shouts of 'Streak'!

Left Shap was one of the finest places to see steam hard at work, and although I came to know it intimately in the latter days of steam, for me it is a place of mixed memories: of days spent camping in the copse opposite Scout Green box (see page 35); an up express in the teeming rain causing a cooked breakfast to be deposited on the floor as it thrashed by the makeshift garage alongside the line; the sheer magic of standing at Shap Wells on a still, frosty morning to see and hear a heavy freight take 25 minutes for the climb to the summit; or desperately sheltering under a wall as it rained horizontally from the west. 24 December 1966 was, however, a pleasant experience in spite of the fact that we left South Yorkshire by car at 05.00! One of the first trains we photographed on that day was a down freight hauled by a then nameless 'Britannia' No 70020 banked by Fairburn 2-6-4T No 42252. The train is seen passing Greenholme under a light covering of snow.

Above A more traditional view at Shap summit. BR Class '4' No 75026 is looped with a trip freight to Harrison's Sidings to allow '8F' No 48421 to pass with a northbound freight. Out of sight beyond the signal box the banker will have dropped off the tail of the freight ready to cross over and return light engine to Tebay. I took only a few photographs on this particular day; the attractions of an invitation of a day's outing on the footplate of the Class '4' far outweighed the possible prospect of a few excellent lineside pictures.

Right One of the more remarkable events of the mid-1960s was the appearance of a Great Western engine at work on lines far from its traditional haunts. For many months there had been rumours that *Clun Castle* might be allowed to work in the north, but few believed it until No 7029 appeared in unusual places for clearance tests. Eventually the 'Castle' managed to find its way to both Carlisle and to Newcastle. In pouring rain and high winds on 14 October 1967 its climbing prowess was tested to the full when it ran north to Carlisle over Shap. The locomotive certainly made a great deal of noise on the approach to Shap summit, but in truth it wasn't performing particularly well. One GW fanatic present soon found an excuse — 'You can't expect the best if you haven't got Welsh steam coal in the tender!'

OVERHEAD
WIRE

Above left Detail of the pony truck of an '8F' 2-8-0. Note the missing builder's plate, already in 1966 a collector's item.

Left A string of Thompson 'B1s' await their next turn of duty at Thornton Junction shed (62A), Fife, in August 1965.

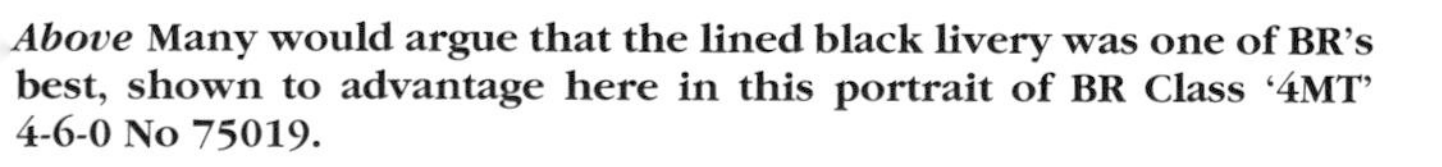

Above Many would argue that the lined black livery was one of BR's best, shown to advantage here in this portrait of BR Class '4MT' 4-6-0 No 75019.

Right Driving wheel detail of 'B1' No 61029 *Chamois*.

Above The old order at Dent. The hard work is over for both engine and fireman as '8F' No 48077 scuttles past the signal box (the picture is taken from the box steps) with a freight for Carlisle on 30 September 1967.

Below Local residents at Edlington near Doncaster today would not recognise this scene of the BR connection into the local colliery of Yorkshire Main. The colliery and all its railway connections have long since gone, including incidentally the huge spoil heap in the background, for many years familiar landmarks of the South Yorkshire landscape. The locomotive is No 63785, one of Robinson's Class 'O4' 2-8-0s rebuilt with a 100A boiler and Thompson cab, a rebuild which rather looked like the proverbial dog's dinner. The replacements look distinctly at odds with the classic lines of its Great Central tender. I was very fortunate in the way the slight wind took the trail of steam from the safety valves behind the locomotive to highlight the chimney and boiler.

Above **Tight fit! The shunter obviously has certain doubts about the clearance as Class 'O4/8' 2-8-0 No 63781 is cautiously eased forward with a loaded coal train from Yorkshire Main to Doncaster Decoy Yard on 4 April 1964. Surprisingly the locomotive carried no lamp code, while the lamps on 'WD' 2-8-0 No 90369 suggest that it was to work a through freight or ballast train, whereas I recall it also worked an unfitted Class 8 coal train. The location of the photograph is the holding sidings on the Great Central and Hull & Barnsley Joint line to Dinnington at Edlington, some 2-3 miles from the colliery complex.**

Right **This heavy engineer's train of new track panels pictured northbound over the Settle & Carlisle on the approach to Ribblehead was clearly a tough proposition even for '17F' of motive power! Both the '8F', No 48742, and '9F' 2-10-0 No 92233 were being worked very hard indeed when this picture was taken on 15 April 1967. I seem to recall a very easy chase by car with the train down to 10 mph or less on parts of the 'Long Drag'. It is noticeable that none of the crew are visible — obviously they were hard at work maintaining a good head of steam.**

Left **The overbridge seen in this picture was an ideal vantage point to get a preview of what was in the shed yard at Holbeck (20A), but on this occasion I was determined to take a few pictures which portrayed the busy scene beneath the bridge. It was the movement of locomotives on and off shed which kept the signalman of Engine Shed Junction box busy. Here, two-tone green Brush Class 47 diesel No D1787 and 'Britannia' No 70017 wait to cross over to the depot while Class '5' No 44662 rattles by with an up freight heading south down the Midland main line.**

Below left **I only ever made two visits to Hartlepool to take railway pictures and it was wet and cold on both occasions; perhaps I would have been more lucky on a third visit. In a steady westerly wind, the drizzling rain highlights the track and the boiler of 'K1' 2-6-0 No 62001 which with No 62008 is busy shunting the Steetly Chemical Works on 9 August 1966. The exact location is Cemetery North Junction; the lines in the foreground were the route to Hetton and Ferryhill.**

Right **Twenty-six Presflos provide an exacting load for '8F' No 48532 pictured hard at work on the 1 in 100 eastbound climb of Norman's Bank to Edale on 8 March 1965. In common with many lines, that in the Hope Valley was plagued by numerous trackside telegraph poles which could make life very difficult for the photographer. Note that here they were, surprise surprise, located in the worst possible place, on the sunny south side of the line!**

Left **The tail-end of a 'WD' 2-8-0, *en route* to Healey Mills yard, makes for an unusual picture at Horbury and Ossett. The swirl of steam was particularly fortuitous.**

Above Ashurst is the first station in the New Forest if you travel by train from Southampton to Bournemouth, and the level crossing there across the A35 road used to create horrendous traffic jams, particularly at weekends. Today a custom-built overbridge has long solved this particular problem, but the route of the old road can be clearly seen in this picture of BR Standard Class '4MT' 2-6-0 No 76061 accelerating away with a Bournemouth–Southampton local train on 25 August 1966. Note the piles of timber ready for shipment, visible to the left of the locomotive.

Below The driver of 'B1' No 61240, formerly named *Harry Hinchliffe*, turns on the power with spectacular effect as it joins the Leeds–Bradford main line at Wortley West with through coaches to Bradford Exchange from King's Cross.

Above The journey from Bradford to Leeds via the old Great Northern route was only 9½ miles, but it was quite an exciting ride. In particular the climbs out of Bradford to Laisterdyke (1¾ miles) and Leeds Central to Armley (2 miles), both at a ruling gradient of 1 in 50, exacted stirring performances from steam engines even when hauling only modest trains of four or five bogies. The falling grade to Wortley West Junction and Leeds is clearly evident in this picture of Fairburn 2-6-4T No 42689 with an eastbound local on 20 August 1966.

Below One of the more glamorous duties for the station pilots at Waterloo was the empty stock workings for the 'Bournemouth Belle'. Ivatt Class '2' No 41298 was in action on this turn late in the afternoon of 16 May 1966. The vantage point for this picture was the top floor of a block of flats, a path well trodden by photographers in the 1960s, much to the chagrin of some of the residents!

Left In the 1990s, in the era of electronically controlled barrier crossings, it seems quite incredible that scenes like this were quite commonplace only 25 years ago. The guard and simple wooden gates were all that protected Class 'J94' No 68012 from the traffic as it crossed the main A5012 Buxton–Ripley trunk road near Pikehall in February 1964.

Below Overdevelopment and overexposure are guaranteed to encourage excessive grain in black and white photography, a technique which emphasises the atmosphere and mood of steam. 'Q6' 0-8-0 No 63407 is silhouetted against the dull grey morning sky on 3 September 1965 as it heads north along the Durham coast towards Blackhall.

Right This train could be heard for a full 10 minutes before it finally loomed into view through the morning mist on the approach to Scout Green. An unidentified Class '5' leads a dead Stanier 2-6-4T (presumed to be *en route* to Troon in Scotland for scrap) on a northbound freight in December 1967.

Below right This photograph was taken at 05.00 after a very uncomfortable night's sleep in the car. Out over the North Sea the sun is just beginning to break through the cloud as an unidentified Class 'J27' attends to a spot of shunting at North Blyth. In spite of my semi-somnolent state, I was lucky in that I had the presence of mind to release the shutter of the camera with the engine and brake-van nicely framed by the footbridge and signal box.

Although this volume is devoted to reminiscences of the days of steam, I thought it would be appropriate to conclude with a recent picture which provides an echo of the past. Many, myself included, thought that steam-hauled trains on our main lines had gone for ever in 1968. Happily many familiar sights have returned although few, perhaps very few, recreate faithfully the scenes of yesteryear. In July 1950 I took this picture of 'Jubilee' *Leander* waiting for the right away from platform 1 at Cudworth near Barnsley with the down 'Devonian'. Little did I realise that just over 30 years later (on 12 December 1981) I would be able to return to almost the same location to photograph the same engine at work on the same track. The earlier photograph was taken from the platform alongside and behind the rear coach. Who knows, I may yet have the opportunity to photograph a GNS 4-4-0 on the main line in Scotland!

Right Heading into the setting sun at Gargrave in the Yorkshire Dales is an '8F' hard at work with a Hunslet–Carlisle freight in September 1965. Ahead is the long slog to Blea Moor and Ais Gill. Alas, scenes like this have gone for ever — the signal box, the station oil lamps and a steam-hauled freight train. R.I.P.

Index